CORPORAL PUNISHMENT IN SCHOOLS: READING THE LAW

Ronald T. Hyman and
Charles H. Rathbone

No. 48 in the NOLPE Monograph Series

DISCLAIMER

The National Organization on Legal Problems of Education (NOLPE) is a private, nonadvocacy and nonprofit association of educators and attorneys. The opinions expressed in this publication are those of the authors and do not represent official views of the Organization.

Published by

NATIONAL ORGANIZATION ON LEGAL PROBLEMS OF EDUCATION
3601 S.W. 29th Street, Suite 223
Topeka, Kansas 66614
(913) 273-3550 • FAX (913) 273-2001

About the Authors

Ronald T. Hyman is Professor of Education in the Department of Educational Theory, Policy and Administration at Rutgers University in New Jersey. A former public school teacher, he earned his doctorate in education from Columbia University in 1965 and his JD from Rutgers University Law School in 1986. He is a member of the New Jersey bar.

Charles H. Rathbone, an educational consultant, is a graduate of Northeastern University School of Law and Harvard Graduate School of Education. A member of the Massachusetts bar, Dr. Rathbone formerly served as a school director in Missouri and as an administrator of teacher preparation programs in both Ohio and Massachusetts.

About the Monograph

The monograph is divided into a preface and two major sections headed Part I and Part II, respectively. Part I analyzes corporal punishment law (procedural due process, substantive due process, cruel and unusual punishment, equal protection, the claim of parental right, civil tort claims and criminal charges) and continues with a discussion of the broader educational and social issues raised by this disciplinary practice. Part II presents an approach to the reading of regulatory language, using illustrative excerpts from actual statues and local policy statements. This section concludes with a compilation of state statutes plus a selection of relevant state case law; these are arranged alphabetically by state.

PREFACE

The nation's attitude toward corporal punishment in schools is in flux. Reform from the right seeks a return to accountability, authority, and an increased demonstration of order in the schools, while reform from the left seeks to create of each school a sanctuary from burgeoning social violence, especially the violence against children that is documented with regularity in the media. At the local level, school board policy is challenged as either too severe or too lenient, while at the state level, a growing number of legislatures are being asked to consider amendments to existing state statutes.

The issues surrounding the use of corporal punishment in schools are several: some are strictly legal, others educational; still others may be characterized as broadly social in their scope. Because no federal statutes address the issue directly and because federal courts have been reluctant to allow constitutional claims, the administration of corporal punishment is generally guided by state law or by regulation of state administrative agencies; often state legislatures delegate authority to the discretion of local school boards or even directly to teachers. In any event, parameters are established within which principals and teachers are *required* to operate. Each educator is also guided, presumably, by *inner* controls — by an educational philosophy, an ethical stance, a practical pedagogy that suggests what will work and what will not to accomplish the school's overall goals.

The intent of this monograph is to assist those wishing to take a closer look at the themes that form corporal punishment policy and at the laws that govern its implementation. To this end, Part I introduces the major legal, social, and educational themes that surround corporal punishment; constitutional challenges to corporal punishment receive particular scrutiny. Part II presents an approach for analyzing regulatory language. It begins with an examination of definitional problems and continues with a series of questions designed to tease apart the separate issues that often become entangled as corporal punishment policy is committed to writing. This section concludes with a state-by-state listing of current statutes and selected case law. Throughout, conventional format has been used for legal citation, though an effort has also been made to avoid legal jargon. All excerpts from actual statutes, regulations, and policy statements are presented precisely as they have been published elsewhere: this leads to an occasional inconsistency of spelling, punctuation, and style that we have not attempted to eliminate. Readers are cautioned to double-check the currency of any statute before relying upon it, since the law in this area is indeed in flux. Most of the legal themes deal with public schools because most cases brought to court challenging corporal punishment are based on laws that prohibit certain *state* actions, and these do not apply to private schools. This does not mean, however, that state laws regulating corporal punishment apply only to public schools: many statutes are written specifically to include both public and independent schools. Moreover, criminal laws and civil tort laws apply in both settings.

TABLE OF CONTENTS

PART I

MAJOR ISSUES AND CONTINUING QUESTIONS

Introduction

School discipline is a persistent problem. When large numbers of children are required by law to attend public school, it is inevitable that some of these children will run afoul of institutional rules. This, in turn, creates a dilemma for the educators in charge. In enforcing school rules, should teachers and administrators employ corporal punishment? In some locations, this is not a permissible option: certain states, counties, and municipal school boards have forbidden the practice.[1] Elsewhere, however, corporal punishment is permitted. Since the underlying friction between individual children and institutional requirements is unlikely to disappear, educators will continue to search for effective means by which to discipline the students they teach. Moreover, if corporal punishment remains an available option, teachers and administrators will continue to test its efficacy. The use of corporal punishment in public schools, however, raises a number of issues. Some of these are legal; others are educational or social in their orientation. All merit close examination.

Legal Issues

The legal issues range wide, and while some might *appear* settled — at least within specific jurisdictions — this is not necessarily the case. For laws can be amended; community standards and public opinion shift; individual judges change. Witness *Brown v. Board of Education*, 347 U.S. 483 (1954), where the Supreme Court overturned its own sixty-year-old "separate but equal" doctrine. Even at the highest judicial level, an apparently settled issue is always subject to review, revision, and occasionally even to reversal.

In the only corporal punishment case to receive its review, the Supreme Court determined that the Eighth Amendment prohibition of cruel and unusual punishment does not apply to schools. *Ingraham v. Wright*, 430 U.S. 651 (1977). Many commentators have

---

1. Although detractors often use the verb, "ban," this is an imprecise term. Even when a state seeks to forbid the practice, questions of scope and effectiveness often remain. Does the prohibition cover private day care and juvenile detention centers? Are student teachers and bus drivers included? Is a teacher who wrongfully punishes a student liable in a civil suit, or is the teacher indemnified? Is the teacher's certificate at risk? These and other complexities argue against using the over-general term, "ban".

concluded that this issue is now closed, but who can say that another group of jurists, weighing a new set of facts at a time when contemporary society has grown ever more sensitive to child abuse, might not decide otherwise? Constitutional reinterpretation or even amendment is always possible; this possibility is part of the rich dynamic of our legal heritage.

Moreover, novel situations continue to arise. Some involve new methodology, as in the case of a nine-year-old student who, while held upside down by her teacher, was stuck by the principal with a paddle so split that "when it hit, it clapped and grabbed." *Garcia v. Miera*, 817 F.2d 650, 653 (10th Cir. 1987). Another recent case involved a second grade teacher who tied a pupil's waist and legs to a chair for the better part of two consecutive days, keeping her from using the bathroom. *Jefferson v. Ysletta Independent School District*, 817 F.2d 303 (5th Cir. 1987). The teacher asserted this was "instructional technique," not corporal punishment. Other cases describe unexpected results of corporal punishment, as when an eight-year-old's arm was broken while he was being paddled. *Crews v. McQueen*, 385 S.E.2d 712 (Ga. Ct. App. 1989). The principal claimed the boy made a twisting movement to avoid a second "lick" of the paddle; the parents asserted the child had been "jerked" up off the floor so hard the arm broke.

The latest novelty involves, not mere differences of technique or outcome, but conflict between coexisting statutes. In Florida, a state statute permitting corporal punishment has come up against child abuse legislation, with teachers caught in the middle.[2] Specifically, section 232.27 of the Florida statutes authorizes corporal punishment, under certain conditions, while Chapter 415 of Florida statute requires the Department of Health and Rehabilitative Services to investigate, report, and prevent child abuse throughout the state. Certain educators who have employed permissible corporal punishment in school have later found themselves listed as child abusers. Some then have sought court order requiring the agency to expunge their names from its registry. They assert that they were acting within the scope of their employment, in conformity with the law authorizing corporal punishment, and within the immunity granted to them

---

2. B.L. and R.W.H. v. Department of Health and Rehabilitative Serv., 545 So. 2d 289 (Fla. Dist. Ct. App. 1989), M.J.B. v. Department of Health and Rehabilitative Serv., 543 So. 2d 352 (Fla. Dist. Ct. App. 1989), B.B. v. Department of Health and Rehabilitative Serv., 542 So. 2d 1362 (Fla. Dist. Ct. App. 1989); *also see* Jaensch, *B.L. and R.W.H. v. Department of Health & Rehabilitative Services: A Denial of Due Process Rights for Teachers*, 19 STETSON L. REV. 689 (1990) and Arkansas Dep't of Human Serv. v. Caldwell, 832 S.W. 2d 510 (Ark. Ct. App. 1992).

by section 232.275 of the Florida statutes. Thus, a conflict has arisen between two state agencies, each claiming support of the law and dedication to children's welfare. These and other cases press courts to consider, and to reconsider, several distinct legal issues that arise from the use of corporal punishment in schools.

1. Protection against cruel and unusual punishment

Does paddling students in school constitute cruel and unusual punishment, if it is excessive or severe? In *Ingraham*, the Supreme Court heard the case of Florida students claiming remedy under 42 U.S.C. section 1983 of the Civil Rights Act of 1871 that school officials under color of state law had violated their Eighth Amendment rights by inflicting upon them cruel and unusual punishment. (Under section 1983, a person or school district acting under color of state law so as to violate a student's Constitutional right is liable for monetary damage.) The case arose on appeal from the Fifth Circuit Court of Appeals. In his 5-4 majority opinion, Justice Powell, himself a former local and state member of Virginia boards of education, held that the Eighth Amendment applies only in criminal contexts and not to civil disciplinary matters involving children in school. Powell argued that the history of the Eighth Amendment, court precedent, the availability of civil and criminal remedies under state law and the general "openness" of schools (as contrasted to the "closed" world of prisons) doomed the students' constitutional claim.

A strong dissent by Justice White challenged Powell's analysis. White took particular issue with the Court's "extreme" view that, "no matter how barbaric, inhumane, or severe," the Eighth Amendment would never properly apply to punishment of a student merely because it was inflicted in a public school setting. *Id.* at 692.

In a critical analysis of *Ingraham*,[3] commentator Rosenberg claims that the Eighth Amendment issue may still be alive, especially in light of White's dissent. Challenging the validity of Powell's dichotomy of "closed" prison and "open" school, she reasons that a student is "not really free to leave school during the day" and that "members of the community are not as welcome to visit the schools as the majority [has] intimated." *Id.* at 86-87. She also points out that Justice Powell has based his reasoning, in part, on the fact that in 1977 there was broad-based national support for corporal punishment. Indeed, only two states then prohibited its use. By contrast, as many as 23 states and most major cities now prohibit or severely limit the use of corpo-

---

3. Rosenberg, *Ingraham v. Wright: The Supreme Court's Whipping Boy*, 78 COLUM. L. REV. 75 (1978).

ral punishment, and bills are pending in numerous state legislatures demanding its abolition.

Moreover, the recent 7-2 Supreme Court decision in **Hudson v. McMillian**, 112 S. Ct. 995 (1992) suggests a possible wedge into the **Ingraham** precedent. In overturning the Fifth Circuit, the **Hudson** court held that "the use of physical force against a prisoner may constitute cruel and unusual punishment [even] when the inmate does not suffer serious injury." *Id.* at 997. Further, "...the Eighth Amendment's prohibition of cruel and unusual punishments 'draw[s] its meaning from the evolving standards of decency that mark the progress of a maturing society,' and so admits of few absolute limitations." *Id.* at 1000 (cites omitted). "The objective component of an Eight Amendment claim is therefore contextual and responsive to 'contemporary standards of decency' **Estelle v. Gamble**, 429 U.S. at 103, 97 S. Ct. at 290." *Id.*[4] Perhaps a future student plaintiff will base a claim on the theory that "serious injury" should no more be an Eighth Amendment threshold in schools than it now is in prisons. Society's growing concern about child abuse, schools' continuing use of corporal punishment, and the Court's recent **Hudson** decision may well lead to a reconsideration of **Ingraham**.

Should the Eighth Amendment be used to protect students as well as criminals from severe corporal punishment? When examining the severity of disciplinary acts, are differences between prisoners and students constitutionally significant? Historically, how has the Eighth Amendment related to other elements of the Constitution, and how **should** it relate? Is Court precedent on the Eighth Amendment all that clear? Do recent changes in the law, in public opinion, and in society itself signal a potential reversal of **Ingraham**? What in fact is the meaning of the Eighth Amendment for today's school children?[5]

---

4. "...Estelle stated the principle underlying the cases discussed in Wilson [Wilson v. Seiter, 501 U.S. ___, 115 L. Ed 2d 271, 111 S. Ct. 2321 (1991)]: punishments 'incompatible with the evolving standards of decency that mark the progress of a maturing society' or 'involv[ing] the unnecessary and wanton infliction of pain' are 'repugnant to the Eighth Amendment.'" Hudson at 1001. Estelle v. Gamble, 429 U.S. 97, 50 L. Ed 2d 251, 97 S. Ct. 285 (1977).

5. For one recent and three older cases on Eighth Amendment claims, *see* Thrasher v. General Casualty Co. of Wis., 732 F. Supp. 966 (W.D. Wis. 1990); Jones v. Parmer, 421 F. Supp. 738 (S.D. Ala. 1976); Gonyaw v. Gray, 361 F. Supp. 366 (D. Vt. 1973); and Ware v. Estes, 328 F. Supp. 657 (N.D. Tex. 1971), *aff'd mem.*, 458 F.2d 1360 (5th Cir. 1972), *cert. denied*, 409 U.S. 1027 (1972).

2. Substantive due process: the protection of liberty and property interests

Does corporal punishment, if excessive, violate a student's liberty rights? If so, what is the appropriate remedy? The right to substantive due process derives from the Fourteenth Amendment, which enjoins states from depriving individuals of life, liberty, or property without due process of law. The essence of substantive due process is protection from arbitrary and unreasonable state action. In *Ingraham*, the Supreme Court never directly considered whether corporal punishment might invade a liberty right under the Fourteenth Amendment, because the court granted *certiorari* review of the Fifth Circuit's *Ingraham* decision only as to the issues of cruel and unusual punishment and procedural due process (Fourteenth Amendment). Nevertheless, Justice Powell noted that "corporal punishment in public schools implicates a constitutionally protected liberty interest...." *Id.* at 672. He further stated that people have the right "to enjoy those privileges long recognized at common law as essential to the orderly pursuit of happiness by free men," which includes the "right to be free from, and to obtain judicial relief for, unjustified intrusions on personal security." *Id.* at 673, *quoting Meyer v. Nebraska*, 262 U.S. 390, 399 (1923) and also citing *Blackstone*.

Though the Court acknowledged that a liberty interest might be violated by excessive corporal punishment, it declined to address the issue directly since "traditional common law remedies are fully adequate to afford due process." *Id.* at 672. In other words, since an aggrieved student may sue an educator in both civil and criminal court under state law, there is no need to provide an additional federal remedy. In dissent, Justice White responded that tort remedies under state law were "utterly inadequate to protect against erroneous infliction of punishment...." *Id.* at 693.

Because the *Ingraham* court declined to address the substantive due process issue, there exists no national standard. Left without guidance, the federal circuit courts, not surprisingly, have been divided. The Fifth Circuit has continued to deny substantive due process claims in corporal punishment cases. In its original *Ingraham* decision, this court set a standard of review: in order for there to be constitutional violation, it held, state action must be found arbitrary, capricious, or wholly unrelated to legitimate state determination of educational policy. *Ingraham v. Wright*, 525 F.2d 909, 916 (5th Cir. 1976), *aff'd on other grounds* 430 U.S. 651 (1977).[6] In *Coleman v.*

---

6. Because this element of the case was not accepted for review by the Supreme Court, it remained the law of the land within Fifth Circuit jurisdiction.

Franklin Parish School Board, 702 F.2d 74 (5th Cir. 1983), the court similarly dismissed the claim of a six-year-old who suffered a head injury after a teacher threw a coffee cup at him. A year later, the court denied the claim of a sixteen-year-old who had been paddled for using abusive language to a school bus driver. *Woodard v. Los Fresnos Independent School District*, 732 F.2d 1243 (5th Cir. 1984). "Corporal Punishment," stated the court, "is a deprivation of substantive due process when it is arbitrary, capricious, or wholly unrelated to the legitimate goal of maintaining an atmosphere conducive to learning." *Id.* at 1246. Four years later, the Fifth Circuit denied the claim of two kindergarten girls who had received a total of five swats each with a wooden paddle from their teachers for snickering. In addition to applying its "arbitrary, capricious and wholly unrelated" standard, the court relied on precedents beginning with *Ingraham* to reject the substantive due process claim, pointing out that "the state of Texas allows for the corporal punishment of children, and provides adequate state criminal and tort remedies for excessive punishment." *Cunningham v. Beavers*, 858 F.2d 269, 270 (5th Cir. 1988)..."

The Fourth Circuit adopted another standard in *Hall v. Tawney*, 621 F.2d 607 (4th Cir. 1980). Reasoning that "substantive due process is concerned with violations of personal rights of privacy and bodily security," the Fourth Circuit found a "right to be free of state intrusions into realms of personal privacy and bodily security through means so brutal, demeaning, and harmful as literally to shock the conscience of a court." *Hall* at 613. Perceiving school punishment and police brutality cases as cognate, the Fourth Circuit established this new standard by drawing on *Rochin v. California*, 342 U.S. 165 (1952) (due process violated where police used stomach pump to force extraction of morphine; this was deemed conduct that shocks the conscience) and on *Johnson v. Glick*, 481 F.2d 1028 (2d Cir. 1973), *cert. denied*, 414 U.S. 1033 (1973) (apart from any "specific" of the Bill of Rights, application of undue force deprives suspect of liberty without due process of law; the same principle should extend to acts of brutality). The court stated,

> [T]he substantive due process inquiry in school corporal punishment cases must be whether the force applied caused injury so severe, was so disproportionate to the need presented, and was so inspired by malice or sadism rather than a merely careless or unwise excess of zeal that it amounted to a brutal and inhumane abuse of official power literally shocking to the conscience.

Hall at 613. With this language, the Fourth Circuit effectively described a three-part condition to define those acts that shock the court's conscience.

The Third Circuit also relied on *Rochin* and *Johnson*. In a case involving a serious disciplinary encounter between a student and a physical education teacher, the court held that the "decision to discipline a student, if accomplished through excessive force and appreciable pain, may constitute an invasion of the child's Fifth Amendment liberty interest in his personal security and a violation of substantive due process prohibited by the Fourteenth Amendment." *Metzger v. Osbeck*, 841 F.2d 518, 520 (3d Cir. 1988). The court then adopted the *Johnson* standard articulated by Judge Friendly of the Second Circuit:

> In determining whether the constitutional line has been crossed, a court must look to such factors as the need for the application of force, the relationship between the need and the amount of force that was used, the extent of injury inflicted, and whether force was applied in a good faith effort to maintain or restore discipline or maliciously and sadistically for the very purpose of causing harm.

Johnson at 1033. This four-part standard resembles the later one established in *Hall* but does not include the "shock the conscience" element which *Hall* took from *Rochin*. Though Judge Friendly omits any "shock the conscience" terminology, he does point out that the *Rochin* standard "gains added content from other language in the opinion. The acts must do more than 'offend some fastidious squeamishness or private sentimentalism about combatting crime too energetically'; they must be such as 'to offend even hardened sensibilities,'... or constitute force that is 'brutal' and 'offensive to human dignity'..." *Johnson* at 1033 (citations of *Rochin* omitted). Based on the four-part Friendly standard, the Third circuit reversed a summary judgment decision in favor of the swimming instructor.

In light of Powell's opinion in *Ingraham*, the Fourth Circuit's decision in *Hall*, and its own decision in *Milonas v. Williams*, 691 F.2d 931 (10th Cir. 1982), *cert. denied*, 460 U.S. 1069 (1983), the Tenth Circuit has held that, "at some degree of excessiveness or brutality," a public school child's substantive due process rights are violated by beatings administered by government-paid school officials." *Garcia v. Miera*, 817 F.2d 650, 655 (10th Cir. 1987), *cert. denied*, 485 U.S. 959 (1988). This is the case where a child, held upside down by her ankles, was hit with "a split board of substantial size on the front of her legs until they bled—supported by evidence of a permanent scar." *Garcia* at 658.

Given the standards established in **Hall, Garcia** and **Metzger**, plus points raised by recent analyses of these cases, the issue of liberty rights appears very much alive, despite the Fifth Circuit's decisions in **Ingraham** and **Woodard**, and despite Justice Powell's Supreme Court remarks on the adequacy of civil and criminal state law remedies.[7] Indeed, one analyst of **Garcia** sees a trend in court decisions that "clears the way for the Supreme Court to declare excessive corporal punishment of school children a violation of substantive due process."[8] Rosenberg also attacks the Fifth Circuit's position as fundamentally irrational. "Rationality is the mainstay of substantive due process analysis," she argues, "[G]overnmental acts must reasonably relate to a permissible objective."[9] Because excessive corporal punishment is both irrational and harmful, and because the Fifth Circuit is "in tension with both Supreme Court decisions and Fifth Circuit cases in other contexts," Rosenberg advocates that the court "should simply do an about-face and join mainstream jurisprudence" on corporal punishment.[10]

Since the Supreme Court has been silent and the circuits are split, several critical questions remain unanswered at the national level: Does excessive corporal punishment violate those liberty interests a student is guaranteed by the substantive due process right of the Fourteenth Amendment? If it does, by what standard shall "severe" or "excessive" be determined? Must punishment literally "shock" the conscience of the court (the Fourth Circuit's **Hall** standard)? Should the standard require prohibited punishments to be "arbitrary, capricious, and wholly unrelated" to the goal of education (the Fifth Circuit's **Woodard** standard)? Should the standard be such that the punishment must meet Judge Friendly's four points (the **Johnson-Metzger** standard)? Should the existence of state civil and criminal remedies for excessive punishment preclude a federal claim under 42 U.S.C. section 1983? How should a federal court assess the sufficien-

---

7. Schlumberger, *Corporal Punishment in the Public Schools: Constitutional Challenge after Ingraham v. Wright*, 31 VAND. L. REV. 1449 (1978); Sweeney, *Corporal Punishment in Public Schools: A Violation of Substantive Due Process?* 33 HASTINGS L.J. 1245 (1982); Rosenberg, *A Study in Irrationality: Refusal to Grant Substantive Due Process Protection Against Excessive Corporal Punishment in the Public Schools*, 27 HOUS. L. REV. 399 (1990).

8. Rhea, *Grossly Excessive Corporal Punishment Violates Students' Substantive Due Process Rights*, 57 MISS. L.J. 237, 252 (1987). *Also, generally, see* Messina, *Corporal Punishment: A Case of Mistaken Identity*, 34 LOY. L. REV. 35 (1988).

9. Rosenberg, *supra* note 3 at 409, *citing* Nebia v. New York, 291 U.S. 502 (1934).

10. *Id.* at 455-456.

cy of state criminal and civil remedies when weighing whether to create a federal remedy? [11]

3. *Procedural due process: the right to notice and to a hearing*

Does corporal punishment in school give rise to a constitutional due process requirement of advance notice and a hearing? The underlying concept of due process is that the state will treat its people fairly; that is, that the laws will be clear and known, and that all citizens may have their day in court. In practice, this right has been reduced to two things, a notice and a hearing. In *Ingraham*, the Supreme Court considered plaintiff's claim that his right under the Fourteenth Amendment's procedural due process clause had been violated. Noting that the "deliberate infliction of corporal punishment" gives rise to a risk that a student's rights will be violated, the court acknowledged that "the child has a strong interest in procedural safeguards that minimize the risk of wrongful punishment and provide for the resolution of disputed questions of justification." *Ingraham* at 676.

Justice Powell then examined available safeguards under Florida law. He argued that common-law remedies were sufficient to deter school officials, since "teachers and school authorities are unlikely to inflict corporal punishment unnecessarily or excessively when a possible consequence of doing so is the institution of civil or criminal proceedings against them." *Id.* at 678. Further, the Court used general criminal law (Fourth Amendment warrantless probable cause arrest) as the appropriate analog to corporal punishment in school — rather than school civil law established in *Goss v. Lopez*, 419 U.S. 565 (1975) (students facing suspension have liberty and property interests that qualify for due process protection).[12] In the end, the Supreme Court denied Ingraham's due process claim, holding that the Due Process Clause "does not require notice and a hearing prior to the imposition

---

11. For some recent cases dealing with substantive due process claims, *see* Wise v. Pea Ridge Sch. Dist., 855 F.2d 560 (8th Cir. 1988); Walchter v. School Dist. No. 14-030, 733 F. Supp. 1005 (W.D. Mich. 1991); Myer by Wyrick v. Litwiller, 749 F. Supp. 91 (W.D. Mo. 1990); Brown v. Johnson, 710 F. Supp. 13 (E.D. Ky. 1989); Cole v. Newton Special Mun. Separate Sch. Dist., 676 F. Supp. 749 (S.D. Miss. 1987); Haverkamp v. Unified Sch. Dist. No. 380, 689 F. Supp. 1055 (D. Kan. 1986); Doe "A" v. Special Sch. Dist. of St. Louis County, 637 F. Supp. 1138 (E.D. Mo. 1986); Hale v. Pringle, 562 F. Supp. 598 (M.D. Ala. 1983); Brooks v. School Bd., 569 F. Supp. 1534 (E.D. Va. 1983); and Rhodus v. Dumiller, 552 F. Supp. 425 (M.D. La. 1982).

12. In *Ingraham*, Powell decides to stick with the point he expressed in his *Goss* dissent rather than to build upon the majority's opinion in that case.

of corporal punishment in the public schools, as that practice is authorized and limited by the common law." *Ingraham* at 682. In short, he argued that state common-law tort laws and criminal laws afford all the due process necessary for a student who is corporally punished. Recently an appellate court used similar reasoning to deny a student's due process claim in *Fee v. Herndon*, 900 F.2d 804 (5th Cir. 1990), *cert. denied*, 111 S. Ct. 279 (1990).

The *Ingraham* court did not distinguish *minor* from *severe* corporal punishment, claiming that the incremental benefit of advance notice and a hearing was not significant. Subsequent analyses by Levin[13] and Rosenberg, together with Justice White's *Ingraham* dissent, suggest otherwise. Justice White contends that "tort action is utterly inadequate." A student can sue only *after* punishment has been inflicted [emphasis added]. Moreover, even if there is a monetary remedy, the "infliction of physical pain is final and irreparable." Due process, on the other hand, provides a "meaningful hedge against the erroneous infliction of irreparable injury." *Ingraham* at 695. Meantime, Levin points out that due process in schools, themselves "large bureaucracies," might actually help improve relationships between teachers and students; fair procedures there might also model the principle of due process being a "deeply embedded" constitutional ideal.[14]

In light of White's dissent and commentators' analyses, questions remain: Should advance notice and a hearing be required prior to the infliction of corporal punishment to protect a student's procedural due process rights under Fourteenth Amendment? To which disciplinary matters does *Goss* rightfully apply? Should advance notice and hearing rights be required only when *severe* punishment is contemplated, or *whenever* corporal punishment is inflicted? What distinguishes severe from ordinary corporal punishment? Should a school be required to notify and hear the parent as well as the child being punished? Are common-law monetary and criminal remedies adequate to compensate a student who has been corporally punished in violation of the Due Process Clause? Do common-law remedies effectively deter educators from using corporal punishment, as claimed by Justice Powell? [15]

---

13. Levin, *Educating Youth for Citizenship: The Conflict Between Authority and Individual Rights in the Public School*, 95 YALE L.J. 1647 (1986).
14. Levin at 1676.
15. For some cases dealing with the "time-out box" and analogous issues, *see* Dickens v. Johnson County Bd. of Educ., 661 F. Supp. 155 (E.D. Tenn. 1987); Hayes v. Unified Sch. Dist. 377, 669 F. Supp. 1519 (D. Kan. 1987); Paul v. McGhee, 577 F. Supp. 460 (E.D. Tenn. 1983); and Glaser v. Marietta, 351 F. Supp. 555 (W.D. Pa. 1972).

4. Equal protection under the law: the claim of discrimination

Can infliction of corporal punishment violate the Equal Protection Clause of the Fourteenth Amendment? While many plaintiffs have claimed violations of the Eighth Amendment and the Fourteenth Amendment's Due Process Clause, few have brought action under the Equal Protection Clause. This is understandable, since a student who sues under the Equal Protection Clause must demonstrate that school officials have implemented their disciplinary policy in a purposefully discriminatory manner or, in an extreme case, that the disciplinary policy explicitly favors one group of students over another. To win on a claim of unequal treatment, plaintiff will first try to convince the court to use a *strict scrutiny* standard by which to assess defendant's behavior. During a strict scrutiny review, defendant must show that the classification employed is *necessary* to achieve a *compelling state interest;* this is a very heavy burden. To qualify for strict scrutiny review, plaintiff must either show that the law being challenged infringes on a right that is constitutionally *fundamental* or that the affected student is a member of a *suspect class.* Certain fundamental rights are enumerated in the Constitution; others have been inferred by the Supreme Court. To date, however, the right to an education has not been so designated.[16] Race has been deemed a suspect class; age and wealth have not. An equal protection action claiming racial discrimination, therefore, would qualify for strict scrutiny review; an action alleging discrimination against rural children or children of a certain age or grade level or against handicapped children would not.[17]

Absent the abridgement of a fundamental right or the employment of a suspect classification (either of which would lead to strict scrutiny), a plaintiff in an equal protection claim will next attempt to convince the court to use an *intermediate level* of scrutiny, one that requires the defendant to show that the classification both serves an *important governmental interest* and is *substantially related* to the achievement of that interest. Gender has been determined to be in this quasi-suspect category. Thus a case involving discriminatory treatment of boys might qualify for this mid-level review.

---

16. Although a parent may have a constitutionally protected family interest in raising and educating children, no child has yet been found to have a fundamental, constitutional right to an education.
17. Determination of suspect classification is rare. Factors for a court to consider include: whether the classification is based upon an immutable characteristic (such as alienage or race), whether the classification has a stigmatizing effect, and whether there has been a history of pervasive discrimination.

Without benefit of strict scrutiny or intermediate level review, any other claim brought under the Equal Protection Clause would be subject to the lowest (*rational basis*) standard of review. Under this standard, a teacher or school system only has to show that the disciplinary policy under which the corporal punishment took place has some rational basis — something along the lines of "helping to create and maintain an atmosphere conducive to learning in the classroom." This burden is the easiest for defendants to meet, especially since courts presume that all statutes have some rational basis, even when not explicitly articulated.

In *Coleman v. Franklin Parish School Board*, 702 F.2d 74 (5th Cir. 1983), a black student claimed discriminatory administration of corporal punishment for a horseplay incident in which a white student also involved was not punished. The teacher allegedly struck the black child with a coffee cup but did not strike the white student. Although the circuit court dismissed the due process claim, it remanded the equal protection claim for further action. [18]

Five years later, in *Cunningham, supra*, after rejecting the substantive due process claim of two kindergarten girls in Texas, the Fifth Circuit went on to consider their equal protection claim. The students contended that they should be viewed as a suspect class or, in the alternative, as members an "at-risk group like women and aliens as a result of their historic mistreatment." They argued this distinction in order to persuade the court to apply strict scrutiny or, alternatively, an "intermediate scrutiny" standard of review. The court rejected these arguments and, applying the rational basis standard, affirmed the district court's decision to reject the girls' equal protection claim. Referring to its 1976 *Ingraham* decision, the Fifth Circuit concluded, "We could not say then, and we cannot say now, that the Texas legislature did not have a rational basis for its legislation." *Cunningham* at 493-494.

In *Cole v. Greenfield-Central Community Schools*, 657 F. Supp. 56 (S.D. Ind. 1986) a hyperactive and emotionally disturbed handicapped student brought suit alleging, in part, violation of his equal protection rights. The court dismissed this claim, commenting that the student "has not established that he is a member of a suspect class, or that any of the interests involved were fundamental pursuant to Equal Protection clause analysis." *Id.* at 63. The court reasoned,

---

18. For three older cases dealing with equal protection on racial discrimination claims, *see* Sims v. Waln, 536 F.2d 686 (6th Cir. 1976), *cert. denied*, 431 U.S. 903 (1977); Sweet v. Childs, 507 F.2d 675 (5th Cir. 1975); and Hawkins v. Coleman, 376 F. Supp. 1330 (N.D. Tex. 1974).

"An elementary school cannot be subjugated by the tyrannical behavior of a nine-year-old child." *Id.*

To date, the Equal Protection Clause has not provided much relief to recipients of corporal punishment. No matter: if plaintiffs feel that an equal protection challenge is the only approach left open at the Supreme Court, they will press the issue, despite a gloomy forecast. Questions to be raised include: Should disparate corporal punishment of various minority groups, handicapped students, and boys be considered violative of the equal protection rights of these students? Should handicapped students, the very young, and boys be considered as members of a suspect or quasi-suspect class? How might "disparate action" by school officials be defined in corporal punishment cases? Should a plaintiff be required to show the school's *intent* to discriminate, or will demonstration of disparate impact on a given class of students suffice, as in Title VII employment cases?[19]

5. The claim of parental right

Should schools have the power to administer corporal punishment without prior approval of the students' parents? Absent that approval, by what authority can it act? Traditionally, schools derived authority from the *in loco parentis* doctrine (literally, "in the place of the parent"). This common law principle gave school officials, serving temporarily in the place of the parent, the right to exercise such authority as a parent would have at home, including authority to administer corporal punishment. Schools were held to the same restrictions as parents: beatings could not be immoderate or wanton or administered with malice or intent to do permanent harm or to inflict serious injury. With the advent of laws requiring compulsory school attendance, however, schools took on an additional and slightly different set of rights and obligations. These derived directly from state power, not indirectly from the rights of parents. By enacting school attendance laws, the state in effect stepped into a new area for which it then acquired both the right and the duty to control. As it gained the right to compel attendance, the state incurred the obligation to deliver a proper education — and if to accomplish this goal the school needed to establish and enforce disciplinary rules, it required no additional statutory mandate to do so.

The interplay of power between parent and state has not been static. A number of state legislatures, apparently concerned about the erosion of *in loco parentis* principles, have enacted new laws that rein-

---

19. Griggs v. Duke Power Co., 401 U.S. 424 (1971).

vest this doctrine with new statutory authority. In Illinois, for instance, the statute reads, "In all matters relating to the discipline in and conduct of the schools and the school children, [educational personnel] stand in the relation of parents and guardians to the pupils...." ILL. REV. STAT. ch 122, para. 34-84a. Here, as in several other states, both lines of authority apply; and since each empowers the state over the individual — the school as arm of the state over the individual parent — the net effect is a reduction in parental power.

Although this tension has yet to be directly addressed by the Supreme Court, Justice Powell does make reference in his *Ingraham* opinion to a summary decision by the Supreme Court in *Baker v. Owen*, 423 U.S. 907 (1975), affirming a circuit court decision that parental approval of the use of corporal punishment is not constitutionally required (although, the court acknowledges, such approval might be required by state law). *Ingraham* at 662. The result of *Baker* and *Ingraham* is an acknowledgement that at times the state's interest in a child apparently overrides a parent's interest. Although in such classic cases such as *Yoder* and *Pierce* the Supreme Court has championed parental rights,[20] in the area of corporal punishment the Court has declined to give parents direct control over what discipline is administered to their children. Parents are permitted only to remove their children from the public school environment, either to enroll them in private school or to teach them at home[21], but thus far they have not been granted the right to veto school policy or to intervene in corporal punishment practice, unless these rights are specifically conferred on them by state law or local policy.

From a parental perspective, the decision of whether or not to use corporal punishment is normally made against a complex backdrop, "a conflux of values with respect to child rearing that may stem from religious, ideological, political, psychological, or ethical consideration."[22] This decision is one of many made out of the same confluence, and it is rarely made in isolation. Those who argue for increased parental influence in school point out that the absence of a veto not only reduces parental authority but often creates a situation

---

20. In Wisconsin v. Yoder, 406 U.S. 205 (1972), the Court held that, under limited conditions, a state's interest in compulsory schooling must give way to the free exercise of religious belief asserted by Amish parents. In Pierce v. Society of Sisters, 268 U.S. 510 (1925), the Court permitted parents to enroll children in non-public but equivalent schools, holding that a state may not require that all children receive instruction from public school teachers only.
21. Both options have considerable economic implication, as they may not be available to those without means.
22. Rosenberg, *supra* note 3 at 107.

in which the student receives dual messages, one from home and the other from school. The conflict of values brought about by this unnatural fragmentation, they claim, is confusing and demoralizing to child and parent alike.[23]

Uncertainty about the ultimate authority of the state to override parental rights raises a number of unsettled questions: Should school officials have the right to inflict corporal punishment on students without specific prior approval by their parents? Should the holding of *Baker* (which considered minor, non-severe corporal punishment) apply to cases involving *severe* punishment? If the Court supports parental rights on issues of religious and sex education, should it find similar ways to support them on corporal punishment? Should a state's right to administer corporal punishment diminish if parental objection is grounded in religious belief? Should parents have the right to demand that school actively employ corporal punishment, even if the school has a policy against using it? How high on the ladder of constitutional values should parental rights be positioned? When should parental interests in a child override the state's?

6. Civil tort claims for excessive punishment

Where civil tort claims are brought seeking damages in state court for excessive corporal punishment, how shall the courts determine what is "excessive"? As Justice Powell noted in *Ingraham*, a student can always seek redress for injuries incurred by suing the teacher or the school district in state court, presumably under theories of negligence or assault and battery. There, the student must demonstrate that excessive force was used, in order to offset defendant's defense that the action was reasonable and lawful.

A key issue is the standard by which a court determines excessive punishment. The Supreme Court of Alabama offers a representative example. It considered the case of an eight-year-old boy who claimed his teacher whipped him with a slat from an apple crate, using excessive force. The teacher claimed that he used only a ping-pong paddle to punish the boy for "insubordination and scuffling in the school hall." The court established five criteria for determining the reasonableness of such punishment: the instrument employed; the nature of

---

23. The parental dilemma seems especially poignant where, generally, the parent is highly supportive of education but, specifically, is very much against the school's corporal punishment policy. In these situations the parent faces an uncomfortable choice — to remain silent and run the risk that the child will assume parental endorsement of this disciplinary practice or to articulate parental disapproval at the risk of undermining the child's confidence in and commitment to school.

the student's offense; the student's age; the student's physical condition; and "other attendant circumstances." To be found guilty of assault and battery, said the court, a teacher "must not only inflict upon the child immoderate chastisement, but he must do so with legal malice or wicked motives or he must inflict some permanent injury." The court held that the teacher's behavior was reasonable, noting medical testimony that there was no permanent injury. *Suits v. Glover*, 71 So. 2d 49, 50 (Ala. 1954).

In Louisiana, an appeals court considered the claim of a fourteen-year-old junior high school boy who sued for damages for a fractured arm and medical expenses, claiming his physical education teacher had used excessive force when punishing him for disrupting instruction. In determining the degree of force permitted, the court ruled that individual facts and environmental characteristics emanating from each case should be considered. This standard is similar to Alabama's, but less specific. The court held that the teacher's "lifting, shaking, and dropping the boy were clearly in excess of that physical force necessary to either discipline or to protect himself. . ." and that the teacher's behavior consequently "subjects the defendants to liability for the injuries incurred." *Frank v. Orleans Parish School Board*, 195 So. 2d 451, 453 (La. Ct. App. Cir. 1967).

No matter what the specific pleading, the plaintiff in a civil case must prove unreasonable force (that is, excessive in terms of the limits established by the state legislature and/or the local school district), as judged by the applicable standard established by the state court. Such a condition makes each decision, as in *Suits* and *Frank*, highly dependent upon the specific facts presented. Because state law is involved, the appropriate standard and the particular definitions of "reasonable" and "excessive" will vary, making generalizations about national standards impossible.

In light of the availability of civil action to remedy improper corporal punishment, a number of questions persist: What should be the state standard for determining whether corporal punishment is reasonable or excessive when it is in some manner permitted? Under what legal theories (e.g., battery, negligence, trespass, false imprisonment) should a civil claim for teacher liability be allowed? Are state remedies adequate to compensate a student for injuries incurred? Do state remedies in fact protect the student's due process rights, as Powell claimed? Should available state civil liability remedies preclude the student from filing a federal due process violation claim under section 1983 of the Civil Rights Act of 1871?

7. Criminal charges for excessive punishment

Where state criminal charges are filed, how shall courts determine what is "excessive?" A crime is an act that violates a state penal code; it represents a public offense. The state imposes a penalty upon those criminally convicted, such as a fine, imprisonment, or removal from office. In prosecuting a teacher for excessive punishment, the state must demonstrate, as in a civil liability case, that the force used was excessive or unreasonable. In a criminal case, however, the state may have to meet a higher standard for determining excessive force. Traditionally, the state must first prove that corporal punishment is a prohibited, criminal act, or that the force used was in excess of what is allowed. It must then show that the teacher in fact punished the student deliberately and that this was done with a criminal state of mind (*mens rea*). In states using the Model Penal Code, the element of *mens rea* has been replaced by four levels of state of mind. These include *purpose or intent* (the highest level), *knowledge, recklessness*, and *negligence* (the lowest level). Unless otherwise specified, a reckless state of mind is minimally required. Because of the state of mind requirement and because of the higher standard for determining excessiveness, it is very difficult to obtain a conviction in corporal punishment cases, especially in states that permit "reasonable" corporal punishment.

A key issue is the standard used for determining reasonableness. In ***People v. DeCaro,*** 308 N.E.2d 196 (Ill. App. Ct. 1974), a state appellate court reversed a trial court's conviction of a sixth grade teacher for the battery of twin boys who had used "obscene and defamatory language" toward him. The court adopted a standard used as early as 1899, stating that the punishment inflicted "was of a traditional nature applied to the traditional place and did not constitute a malicious or wanton disregard for the physical welfare of the boys. ..." *Id.* at 198. The court noted that even if the punishment had been excessive, defendant would be innocent because he "was acting within his authority and did not act in a malicious or wanton manner." *Id.*

In another case brought seven months later under the same law, the Illinois Supreme Court held that "teachers should be subject to the same standard of reasonableness which has long been applicable to parents in disciplining their children." ***People v. Ball***, 317 N.E.2d 57 (Ill. 1974). The teacher was judged guilty of battery of an eleven-year-old boy and fined $100 plus costs. This decision negated the "malicious and wanton" standard used earlier in ***DeCaro,*** replacing it with a "parental reasonableness" standard. This was then used by another Illinois court to convict a principal of accountability in the corporal punishment of a twelve-year-old. *People v. Wehmeyer*, 509 N.E.2d 605 (Ill. App. Ct. 1987).

In *State v. Hoover* 450 N.E.2d 710, (Ohio Ct. App. 1982), the Ohio Court of Appeals held that, in light of a recently-enacted criminal statute, the state "must prove not only the elements of assault...but also must prove beyond a reasonable doubt that the corporal punishment was unreasonable and was not reasonably necessary to preserve discipline." *Id.* at 714. Based on this standard, the court reversed a lower court's conviction of an assistant superintendent convicted of a criminal assault for corporally punishing a student.

A slightly different standard was applied to New York's definition of assault in the third degree in *People v. Baldini*, 159 N.Y.S.2d 802 (1957). Quoting penal code section 246 (4) that force is not unlawful if it is "reasonable in manner and moderate in degree," the court noted approvingly that statutes then applicable in New York permitted corporal punishment and that even the "Bible sanctions same." *Id.* at 806. The court found no malice on the part of the teacher, that the actions of the teacher did not warrant conviction of assault in the third degree, and that the teacher's guilt was not proven beyond a reasonable doubt for slapping a student with the open hand on the cheek when the boy refused the teacher's direction.

Although the standard used to assess criminal charges will vary from state to state, in general it is more difficult to convict a teacher criminally than civilly because criminal codes set high standards, especially as to burden of proof and state of mind. As a result, fewer criminal charges are filed. In light of the availability of criminal action, certain questions remain: What should be the state standard and requirements for convicting an educator for the crime of excessive corporal punishment? What should the penalties be? Are existing remedies sufficient both to punish and to serve as deterrence? Should the availability of criminal action preclude a student from filing a federal due process claim under section 1983 of the Civil Rights Act of 1871?

Educational and Social Issues

Western society has long believed that children need a strong hand to guide them to appropriate behavior. For centuries, parents have spanked children for misbehavior and have tolerated, if not encouraged, their teachers doing the same. In justification, both parents and teachers have cited religious authority: "Spare the rod and spoil the child," for example.[24] For some, corporal punishment may retain its original religious purpose — to beat sin out of the child and thus to cleanse the soul.[25] For many, however, corporal punishment is simply seen as a useful and acceptable way to teach children proper behavior. It teaches moral values (tell the truth; do not cheat) and sets social expectations (line up quietly; obey your teacher). It is swift and memorable, an immediate and palpable reminder, delivered on the spot and in terms that children well understand. Although its physical effect is transitory, the lesson is lasting. Along these lines New York's Mayor David Dinkins recently described a whipping he received at the age of nine at the hands of his mother and grandmother for having stolen reflectors with which he wanted to decorate his skate-scooter. He remarked, "They took all my clothes off, stood me in the bathtub and beat me with straps. I have not stolen a reflector since."[26]

Some educators believe that spanking and paddling, as well as non-striking punishment such as washing the mouth with soap, exhaustive exercise, isolation in a classroom corner or dark closet, and gagging, are effective devices for behavior modification. When a student learns to associate inappropriate behavior with strong negative consequences, that student will quickly modify the undesirable behavior to conform with educational and social norms. Corporal punishment thus becomes a direct, effective way to establish control over a misbehaving student and to send an unambiguous message about the unacceptability of certain behavior and the degree of a teacher's disapproval. For proponents, corporal punishment is viewed as a useful technique that is educationally sound and morally just. It punctuates the critical lesson that all must learn in order to

---

24. *Proverbs* 22:15 (*King James*) "Foolishness is bound in the heart of a child; but the rod of correction shall drive it from him." 23:13-14 "Withhold not correction from the child: for if thou beatest him with the rod, he shall not die./ Thou shall beat him with the rod, and shall deliver his soul from hell." 13:24 "He that spareth his rod hateth his son: but he that loveth him chasteneth him betimes." The precise phrasing of the adage seems to come from Venning, Mysteries and Revelations (1649) which was based, in turn, on the Athenian dramatist, Meander. *See also* Samuel Butler's poem, "Hudibras," (Part II, Canto I, Line 843): "Love is a boy, by poets styl'd; Then spare the rod and spoil the child" (1664). For more on the origins of fundamentalist belief, *see* Greven, SPARE THE CHILD: THE RELIGIOUS ROOTS OF PUNISHMENT AND THE PSYCHOLOGICAL IMPACT OF PHYSICAL ABUSE (1991) and I. Hyman [no relation], READING, WRITING, AND THE HICKORY STICK: THE APPALLING STORY OF PHYSICAL AND PSYCHOLOGICAL ABUSE IN AMERICAN SCHOOLS (1990).
25. According to Greven, the threat of future and eternal punishment is embedded in most Christian theology; it represents "one of the greatest sources of anxiety and terror ever known, and must be recognized as the primary basis for the rationales for painful physical discipline and punishment...." Greven at 60.
26. N.Y. Times, September 21, 1990 at B-3.

live in an orderly society — that each of us must at times suppress our individual urges and do what is right for the greater good of society, as interpreted by those in authority.

The rationale for prohibiting corporal punishment is equally straightforward. Opponents assert that corporal punishment does more harm than good. Psychologically it is damaging, they contend, and educationally it is unsound. Though the use of fear, pain, and humiliation may compel obedience in the short run, the long-term consequences are that the children turn angry at everything connected with school, that they become aggressive in the classroom, and that they continue to behave violently outside the school context. Alternatively, they become timid, cowed, beaten — unwilling to risk anything new, unimaginative and dull.[27] Medically, opponents note, corporal punishment can result, not only in superficial contusions, but in Post Traumatic Stress Disorder, a disability normally associated with the psychological aftermath of war, natural disaster, rape, and other types of mega-violence. Moreover, corporal punishment impedes and perhaps even negates other educational objectives. To the extent that education favors independence and personal responsibility, the internalization of social values and self-motivation, belief in the intrinsic joy and usefulness of all learning, a preference for cooperation, a belief in democracy and joint decision-making, and respect for the thoughts and feelings of others within a social group, corporal punishment is counterproductive. It teaches instead the value of aggressive physical action as a means of settling problems and relies on brute force by the powerful over the weak. It undercuts the image of teacher as exemplar of reasoned behavior, nurturing adult and creative problem-solver.[28]

Citing data that indicate that poor and minority students receive more corporal punishment than their white, middle-class classmates,[29]

---

27. According to some, the problems corporal punishment is often called upon to solve are of the teacher's own making. Boredom, resistance to irrelevant material, and the strain of physical inactivity are attributable to poor classroom management, inappropriate curriculum and unimaginative teaching, they claim.

28. Opponents also point out the low cost/benefit ratio of using this approach. On the one hand, corporal punishment is associated with poor academic achievement [Ashwick, SCHOOL DISCIPLINE POLICIES AND PRACTICES, September, 1986 BULLETIN OF THE OFFICE OF EDUCATIONAL RESEARCH AND IMPROVEMENT 1, 4 (1986)]; on the other, it presents a serious risk of court action for teacher and school. The time, cost, and general aggravation of defending a lawsuit can so sap the resources and good will of a school district that it becomes unsound educational management to continue using this means of discipline.

29. Nationwide, minority students, who make up 30 percent of the total 41.1 million students in public schools, account for 40 percent of the 1.1 million corporal punishment cases in 1986. N.Y. Times, August 16, 1990 at 1.

opponents charge that corporal punishment is typically applied in a discriminatory manner. Handicapped students, boys, and rural pupils in small schools all appear to receive a disproportionate share of physical discipline, they assert.[30]

A final argument is that, to some, corporal punishment is morally objectionable. It is a form of violence, and violence in any form is wrong, especially wrong when used by older and larger adults against younger and weaker children. According to this position, teachers simply ought not to be allowed to commit acts that, elsewhere in society, would be considered at the very least abusive and possibly criminal. Thus corporal punishment undermines the moral authority of the entire educational enterprise.

Whether corporal punishment works, the speed and duration of its effectiveness, how well this approach coordinates with other school policy: these questions are essentially pedagogical. Some persons, however, believe that the use of corporal punishment raises issues that transcend its school context. Whether or not intended, school serves as a model of society: it is a highly visible indicator of the values and policies of the society it serves. At times the school leads; at times it follows; often it does both. For this reason, corporal punishment is perceived as symbolic; both its proponents and its opponents see its effect as being of longer duration and of greater impact than merely bounded by the school day and school calendar. Those concerned about violence in American society, for example, see corporal punishment as a dangerous contribution to that violence, while those concerned about the erosion of the social order see corporal punishment as an important means of bringing order into the lives of otherwise undisciplined children.[31]

---

30 According to Ashwick (*supra* note 22), junior high schools use corporal punishment more than high schools at a ratio of 52% - 37%, small schools more than large schools at a ratio of 51% - 26%, and rural schools more than urban at a ratio of 58% - 27%. Ashwick *passim*. Elsewhere is has also been contended that handicapped children are struck more often than non-handicapped. N.Y. Times, August 16, 1990 at B-12. For an interesting case involving a handicapped student, *see* Department of Health and Rehabilitative Serv. v. School Bd. of Hillsborough County, 557 So. 2d 40 (Fla. Dist. Ct. App. 1990). *See also* Nelson and Siegel, *Corporal Punishment and Handicapped Children*, 64 FLORIDA B.J. 43 (1990).

31 Acknowledgment of the social significance of corporal punishment may depend upon whether one approves or disapproves its use. Since opponents have been more prolific in their commentary than proponents, criticism generally outweighs advocacy, both in quantity and in the degree to which certain positions have been articulated.

Clearly, the country is divided about the role of corporal punishment.[32] Slightly more than half the states currently allow some degree of corporal punishment, and recent polls reflect this split: in 1988, 50% of the American public approved of "spanking and similar forms of physical punishment in the lower grades of some schools for children who do not respond to other forms of discipline," while 45% disapproved and 5% did not know. Among teachers (in 1989), the figure for approval was 56%, with 38% disapproving and 6% without a clear opinion.[33] This division of policy and attitude conveys a confusing message. Children, parents, teachers, and administrators, especially if they move from school to school or from state to state, encounter enormous variations of policy and practice. While to some this is merely a reflection of life in a pluralistic society or a manifestation of the political power of certain groups at certain times in the formulation of local policy, others see worse. They see moral confusion, legislative laziness, indifference to children. Either way, the ambiguity raises a number of challenging questions about society in general and about social policy in particular.

1. Should there be a national policy on corporal punishment?

Uniformity of practice would certainly eliminate much confusion:[34] everyone would know what to expect, while legislatures and school boards would be off the hook on this politically divisive issue. Those involved in teacher education could develop both pre-service and in-service programs to clarify teacher expectation and refine practical detail. Over time, jurisdictional differences would diminish, as different courts in different states would look to one another in developing consistent approaches to the application of identical law.[35] For those whose position on this subject was adopted, there would be total vic-

---

32. If current policy reflects what society wants (an untested assumption), this may suggest that pockets of uniformity exist, with differing geopolitical units taking opposite positions. Alternatively, it could mean that slim majorities have prevailed over significant minorities on this issue.

33. Elam, *The Second Gallup/Phi Delta Kappa Poll of Teachers' Attitude Toward the Public Schools*, 70 PHI DELTA KAPPAN 785, 787 (1989).

34. Numerous nations have forbidden the use of corporal punishment. Some representative countries of western Europe include (showing year of enactment): Poland (1783), Italy (1860), France (1881), Norway (1936), Portugal (1950), Germany (1970), Ireland (1982). Messina at 44.

35. Had Justice White prevailed in *Ingraham* or had a similar case come before the Warren court a few years earlier when the Supreme Court was actively expanding civil rights and civil liberties in many analogous areas, the nation might well have had a *de facto* policy today, according to some observers.

tory; no minority viewpoint could be maintained without replicating the present uncertainty and contradiction.

The arguments against the formulation of a national policy speak to the benefits of home rule, a long-standing tradition of local control over education, and acknowledgment of sincerely-held differences of opinion on this subject. Honoring the diversity that both enriches and reflects life in a pluralistic society, this view also cautions against monolithic governmental intrusion of any sort. It warns that if nation-wide policy on this controversial practice is imposed upon those who disagree with it, other policies might follow. Both those in favor and those opposed worry about losing in an all-or-nothing national struggle.

2. *Where corporal punishment is allowed, who should police its administration?*

Out of a tradition of checks and balances comes the adage, "Don't send a fox to guard the chickens." Though schools are not as totally isolated as prisons or asylums,[36] they are not altogether open to the public view; and the argument can be made that, as with any group of workers, members of a teaching staff will tend to close ranks, tolerate deviate behavior by one of their own, and generally be more forgiving of their own membership than an outsider charged with monitoring their conduct might be.

In Florida, the state legislature mandated the Department of Health and Rehabilitative Services (DHRS) to monitor all child abuse in the state. Child abuse is defined in section 415.503 (3) of the Florida Statutes as "harm or threatened harm to a child's physical or mental health or welfare by the acts or omissions of the parent or other person responsible for the child's welfare." DHRS set specific guidelines to permit objective detection of child abuse. Among the criteria to be used was any bruise lasting over 24 hours that had been made by a paddle during corporal punishment. Such bruising was sufficient evidence, they determined, that the paddling was excessive. Using that definition, DHRS investigated 820 public school employees from July, 1988 to June, 1989: they then confirmed 71 as child abusers.[37] The names of these individuals were later placed on a special list of "child abusers" who, because of this designation, were disqualified from working with children and from certain other posi-

---

36. On the characteristics of total institutions such as mental hospitals, prisons, and army camps, *see* Goffman, Asylums (1961).
37. Education Week, October 11, 1989 at 17; N.Y. Times, September 24, 1989 at 23.

tions dealing with the developmentally handicapped, the aged, and disabled adults.

As a result of several lawsuits, DHRS later refined its basic defini-tion. According to a March 16, 1990 Inter-Office Memorandum, "'excessive corporal punishment' means inflicted punishment which results in an injury that is deemed to be excessive and investigation does not reveal contrary evidence, i.e., self defense, injury not inflicted during corporal punishment or the parents can supply evidence of a medically-documented blood disorder or other evidence that the child is abnormally susceptible to bruising. The length of time that a bruise is visible is now only one factor to consider in determining whether the punishment was excessive. The totality of the circum-stances must be examined to arrive at such a definition."

The Florida situation illustrates the complexity of establishing a watchdog-type agency to oversee activity that goes on within schools. Even if DHRS and the Department of Education were to agree on what behavior is permissible, there is always the likelihood of inter-agency conflict over interpretation. In this instance, most of the teachers had acted in a manner permitted by the state's corporal pun-ishment laws: it was the laws pertaining to child abuse that got them into trouble. With or without a watchdog agency, the problems of adequate monitoring are imposing.

3. What is the proper role of school in a changing society?

In a dynamic society, the elements of change and the elements of stability are ever in tension. As an institution responsible for the socialization of youth, the school can act either as conservator of out-moded social norms or as change agent and teacher of the newest fashion. Usually it functions somewhere in the middle. Whether a school leads or lags is both a matter of perception and a matter of policy, but the stakes invariably rise when any particular issue is per-ceived to be grounded in a fundamental value. For those who relate corporal punishment to such bedrock, school practice immediately appears critical: it is as though a building inspector has detected radon or asbestos. For those who fail to ascribe such significance, the situation is more like discovering a leak in the roof — it should undoubtedly be fixed, but children's lives are not at stake. As with other controversial school topics (e.g., sex education, religion, and politics), corporal punishment has the potential for highlighting grander questions about the role of school in society.

4. As changes occur in corporal punishment policy, where are the likely sources of power and leadership?

Corporal punishment policy is changing. From district to district and from legislature to legislature, policies are being articulated, debated, and voted upon. Though voices tend to be shrill on this issue, results are quite mixed: though many states have all but eliminated corporal punishment from their schools, others have clarified teachers' authority to use force and to take such disciplinary action as would be permitted the absent parent. For those interested in accelerating change in current corporal punishment policy, the courts are not perceived as particularly receptive as agents of change. Since *Ingraham* in 1977, federal courts have appeared reluctant to support constitutional claims in this area, while state courts, restricted for the most part to interpreting state law, have tended to defer to the legislative will. Teacher organizations and professional groups of school administrators have been remarkably silent on the subject,[38] and though other professional organizations have taken stands (usually in opposition), none has given the topic an especially high priority.[39] While occasionally a political leader will step forward on this issue, executive leadership is usually confined to positions taken within state agencies. Privately-operated public interest groups have been loud, but not especially effective.[40]

This leaves state legislatures as the most likely locus of change. Even there, however, things do not always proceed as planned. The *Winston-Salem Journal* of July 7, 1991 reports how students in an advanced political science seminar at the University of North Carolina responded to an assignment to draft a bill to be presented to a state legislator during their forthcoming field trip to the state capital. One group interested in eliminating corporal punishment pro-

---

38. The National Education Association, the American Federation of Teachers, and the American Association of School Administrators, for example, do not have stated policies on the issue of corporal punishment.
39. Professional organizations that have taken a stand against corporal punishment are too numerous to list. Their memberships represent medical (American Medical Association), legal (American Bar Association), public interest (National Association for the Advancement of Colored People, American Civil Liberties Union), and educational (Association for Supervision and Curriculum Development) interests; most of these groups have voted formal resolutions on the subject.
40. Such groups include: The National Coalition to Abolish Corporal Punishment in Schools (of Columbus, OH); The Committee to End Violence Against the Next Generation (of Berkeley, CA); The National Center for the Study of Corporal Punishment and Alternatives in the Schools (of Temple University in Philadelphia, PA).

posed a bill, not to abolish the practice, but to give local school districts the option to set their own policy, since earlier state statute had forbidden such practice. After some six months of lobbying, the bill passed. Although the students made their argument on moral grounds, the legislators passed the bill largely as a way of dropping this "hot potato" issue back down on local school boards. Though the result pleased the students, the political lesson was undoubtedly unexpected.

5. What is the rightful position of children in American society, and how can corporal punishment policy best reflect this position?

Children in this country are afforded certain rights and privileges: they are spared economic oppression by child labor law; they enjoy numerous protections within the judicial system; they have the right to a free public education; they may not be abused. At the same time (and perhaps for the same reason), children have traditionally been subject to greater state control than other citizens; their right to an education, for example, is balanced by the obligation of compulsory attendance. The inevitable tension between right and responsibility, between freedom and control, plays out for this particular group over the issue of corporal punishment, with detractors reading the situation one way and proponents another.

Though compulsory attendance and social isolation are also the lot of soldiers, prisoners, and mental patients, these groups are protected from physical discipline in ways that school children are not. Whether this is intentional or an anomaly, the differential treatment raises questions about the relative status of the child in the larger society, the significance accorded bodily integrity of the young, and the differing rights of a state *vis-à-vis* its various citizens.

Before parents, educators, or attorneys can become successful participants in the shaping of corporal punishment policy, it is essential that they comprehend the full scope of all laws and regulations currently in effect. To this end, Section Two introduces an analytical approach to assist in the careful reading of regulatory language likely to be encountered.

PART II
READING THE LAW:
PRELIMINARY QUESTIONS

Definitional Difficulties

Good definitions of corporal punishment permit all concerned to know which acts are sanctioned and which are not. Teachers and administrators, parents and attorneys, judges, juries, the press, even the children involved — all profit from definitions that create a clarity of understanding on which all parties may rely. Unfortunately, the formulation of good definition is rare. This is partly political, partly due to differences of interpretation as to what the term should ultimately include, and partly it is because of the legislative context in which the words are being used. Although political analysis is beyond the scope of this study, suffice it to say that public policy is often the product of compromise, and statements attempting to express such policy are often themselves patchwork. It may also be true that for legislators who do not have the votes to get their way, generalization and opacity appear preferable to the absolute clarity of an unsatisfactory policy.

To appreciate the complexities involved in formulating an effective definition, it is helpful to examine several currently in force, and also to demonstrate how any particular definition can be tested, through its application to hypothetical situations that emphasize its inadequacies. One straightforward definition of corporal punishment in a school setting might be: *Corporal punishment consists of an act of punishment taken by a teacher, that intentionally causes physical harm to a student's body.* While this definition is sufficient to encompass the situation in which a teacher paddles a student three times for willful disobedience of a rule against spitting, it proves less helpful in other instances.

Suppose, for example, that eight-year-old Tom has grown a short ponytail in imitation of adult relatives and his rock star idols. School officials determine that this hair style violates the school's dress and grooming code and direct him to cut it off. Tom refuses. The principal then places Tom in a separate, 6' x 9' room where he remains all day, learning his lessons and eating his lunch in solitude. Tom feels that he has been put in jail. Does this placement — confining a child to a small room for disobeying a school rule — constitute corporal punishment?

Or suppose that Dick disobeys his teacher by getting up every few minutes to sharpen his pencil. As punishment, the teacher tethers the child to his assigned seat with a jump rope. Now Dick cannot move about the classroom whenever he wishes, disrupting others. Is this corporal punishment? Would it make a difference if Dick were very loosely tied? What if the rope were tight, leaving marks that hurt?

Finally, suppose that, because she has punched another student at recess, eleven-year-old Harriet has been ordered to sit at the front of the class all afternoon on a stool. The seat of the stool is only six inches in diameter and is decidedly uncomfortable. Would this qualify as corporal punishment under the above definition? Would it make a difference if the seat were larger, thus fitting Harriet's buttocks better? Would it matter if the punishment occurred off to the side of the classroom, rather than in full public view?

Physical punishment which is directly inflicted falls under nearly any definition of corporal punishment: the use of a switch, a paddle, even a bare hand are palpably physical, requiring force to administer, leaving marks on the skin and causing obvious and immediate pain to the recipient. In the situations of Tom, Dick and Harriet, however, the situation is less clear. Where there is mere restraint and no external blow or where the pain, even if physical, is essentially internal (stiffness or sore muscles), or where the distress is principally emotional (humiliation or fear), then a question arises as to whether the punishment is genuinely *corporal*.

A review of current state law and local school board policy reveals enormous diversity on this point. Whether forbidding or permitting corporal punishment, present state and local definitions themselves range from the very general to the highly specific. Here, for example, are two general definitions:

> "Corporal punishment is defined as inflicting physical hurt upon a student in order to punish him for misconduct." (Orangeburg County School District No. 5, South Carolina)

> "...'corporal punishment' means the deliberate infliction of physical pain by any means upon the whole or any part of a pupil's body as a penalty or punishment for a pupil's offense." (MICH. COMP. LAWS ANN. §380.1312)

Note that the Michigan statute includes the open-ended phrase, "by any means." Under this law, one could claim corporal punishment for Tom, Dick, and Harriet, providing "deliberateness" was also proved. Other statutes, while intending a similar inclusiveness, present lists of defining behavior:

> "'Corporal punishment' includes but is not limited to paddling, slapping or prolonged maintenance of physically painful positions, when used as a means of discipline." (WIS. STAT. ANN. §118.31)

To illustrate an even higher degree of specificity, there follows a statute that provides illustrative particulars for one of its own defining phrases:

> "Corporal punishment is defined as the infliction of bodily pain for disapproved behavior. However, in the definition of corporal punishment it is necessary to include under the phrase, 'infliction of bodily pain,' not only striking, but any action which seeks to induce bodily pain, for example, forcing the student to stand on tip toes with finger-tips outstretched against the wall, or to crouch or bend over and remain in such painful cramped positions for long periods of time, or to run laps around the building or in the gym until exhausted, etc." (Southfield, Michigan School Board)

As a variation on this theme of specificity, some definitions carefully distinguish permissible from impermissible corporal punishment, defining either or both. For example:

> "'Corporal punishment' does not mean: (B) Physical pain or discomfort resulting from or caused by voluntary participation in athletic competition or other such recreational activity, voluntarily engaged in by a pupil." (OR. REV. STAT. ANN. §339.250)

> "No cruel or unusual form of corporal punishment shall be inflicted upon any student, including but not limited to restraint by binding arms, legs, or torso, washing out the mouth with soap and verbal abuse." (Yakima Public Schools, Washington)

Note that this last definition would prohibit the jump-rope tethering of Dick (though not the confinement of Tom). Similarly, the "prolonged maintenance of physically painful positions" language of the Wisconsin statute would prohibit placing Harriet on the stool.

Such increased specificity often enlarges the scope of what is defined as corporal punishment — although case law suggests that the variety of punishment techniques available to the inventive teacher approaches the infinite and that no detailed list, no matter how comprehensive, could expect to cover all eventualities. (Teachers have been taken to court for using cattle prods, curtain rods, pins, and all manner of unpredictable instruments in the service of corporal punishment.)

Occasionally, a law will specify in its definition of corporal punishment, not only a particular act, but the *threat* of that act:

> "School employees are also prohibited from employing threats either expressed or implied of corporal punishment. This includes the display of devices such as paddles or sticks normally associated with corporal punishment." (Southfield, Michigan School Board)

To the extent that a threat is often less obvious than an overt physical act, the supervision and enforcement of regulations involving threats obviously become problematic. Thus a definition can itself set up certain problems in its subsequent application. This is also true when the definitional focus shifts from the act of the punisher to the effect of that act upon the recipient. Consider, for example, the Minnesota statute that states:

> "...corporal punishment means conduct involving (2) unreasonable physical force that causes bodily harm or substantial emotional harm." (MINN. STAT. §127,45)

While acknowledging the importance of emotional harm to children as well as the potential affective consequences of an otherwise purely physical experience, the Minnesota legislature has produced a definition that, because it relies on terms that themselves require further definition, does little to enhance predictability. For some, this is viewed as simply impractical: the statute cannot be enforced without additional guidance on what constitutes "substantial emotional harm." For others, this awkwardness is perceived as the inevitable consequence of the inherent unpredictability of emotional matters and a brave commitment to the protection of those who suffer, even though the suffering cannot always be accurately forecast. Perhaps this type of definition works better in places — like Minnesota — where corporal punishment has been proscribed and where such language merely extends the coverage (or the threat of coverage), but is not required to serve as a basis for drawing precise lines between permissible behavior and impermissible.

Concentration upon the subjective, recipient-baséd outcome rather than on the objective, behavioral act of the punisher was addressed by a California official who wrote:

> "It is the causing of pain which is prohibited — not the particular method or methods by which it is caused." (Letter from California Deputy Attorney General Van Wye, 1988)

This is an instance where interpretation of a regulation rather than statutory language itself places emphasis upon *effect*.

Ultimately, of course, "corporal punishment" as a legal term is what the courts say it is, and if the statute, regulation, or policy statement proves difficult to interpret, then there will be a wide variety of interpretations until, at any given level of authority, someone or some body makes a definitive, precedent-setting interpretation. Absent explicit statutory language defining corporal punishment, courts will inevitably rely on what they believe to be "common understanding" of the term, and this returns everyone to square one! And of course, the more abstract or general or vague the basic definition, the more discretion will flow to the interpreter. A school board rule from Yakima, Washington illustrates this dilemma:

> "No cruel or unusual form of corporal punishment shall be inflicted upon any student including but not limited to... verbal abuse." (Yakima, Washington Public Schools)

Surely this definition stretches the "corporal" aspect of corporal punishment as far as it can reasonably be stretched.

The question of *intentionality* is also germane. Must a teacher intend for the child to experience pain for the punishment to constitute corporal punishment? What if the pain is inadvertent? Suppose Harriet's teacher never considered the size of the stool or that she never intended for the child to sit there for three unrelieved hours? Would this unintentional causing of pain nonetheless constitute corporal punishment? Or suppose that Dick's teacher did not mean to tie the rope so tightly or that Tom's principal never knew that the child suffered from claustrophobia, never knew that *for this child* this particular form of punishment would become a terrifying, body-threatening ordeal?

Many statutes on corporal punishment simply include such a word as "intentional" or "deliberate" or "willful" and define its meaning no further:

> "...'corporal punishment' means the intentional infliction of physical pain which is used as a means of discipline" (WIS. STAT. ANN. §118.31)

"...'corporal punishment' means the willful infliction of, or willfully causing the infliction of, physical pain on a pupil." (CAL. EDUC. CODE §49001)

"...'corporal punishment' means the deliberate infliction of physical pain by any means...as a penalty or punishment for a pupil's offense." (MICH. COMP. LAWS ANN. §380.1312)

Those given the task of interpreting a teacher's behavior as to whether or not it was "intentional" derive little guidance from such language: they must rely, not on any clues from the statute, but rather on common usage, or what a "reasonable person" would understand by the term. And even if a legislature did attempt to define these terms, what words would it use? Owing to its inherent subjectivity, intent is notoriously difficult to prove, no less to define.

The issue of intentionality intersects with the question of whether or not the regulation places its focus on the behavioral act itself or on the effect of the act. To the extent that corporal punishment is defined by the reaction it evokes, intentionality, it might be argued, becomes irrelevant. For if the focus is on the physical injury, or on the pain, or on the ensuing nightmares, then one might argue that the specifics of cause are of no consequence. This argument breaks down, however, when the call for intentionality is specifically linked to the original, physical act — rather than linked to the effect. "Did she mean to strike the student in the first place?" is a very different question from, "Did she intend for the student to suffer injury, pain or emotional distress?"

It should also be noted that some definitions specifically exclude the stress and pain associated with athletic endeavor:

"This definition shall not include physical pain or discomfort caused by participation in practice or competition in an interscholastic sport, or participation in physical education or an extracurricular activity." (VA. CODE ANN. §22.1-279.1)

"...'corporal punishment' does not mean: (B) Physical pain or discomfort resulting from or caused by participation in athletic competition or other such recreational activity, voluntarily engaged in by a pupil." (OR. REV. STAT. ANN. §339.250)

Statutes like these are intended to protect coaches who order students to perform calisthenics and other exercises that "hurt." Note the differences between these two statutes, however: the Oregon statute excludes from its definition of corporal punishment only *voluntary* activities. This raises an interesting question: under this statute, would the same behavior that is permissible for a coach of a voluntary team become impermissible corporal punishment if engaged in by the same individual during a compulsory gym class?

Finally, any workable definition must consider the basic meaning of *punishment.* Generally, punishment is taken to mean a retributive consequence imposed by a person in authority upon someone for prior improper behavior. But what of the situation in which the teacher claims an *educational* justification for the act? Suppose, for example, that Tom's teacher asserts that this particular student has always worked better in isolation, that otherwise he becomes too easily distracted by the other children. Or suppose an instance in which a teacher inadvertently causes corporal harm while intending something quite different. Suppose at the start of recess the teacher directs all students to run around the perimeter of the playground in order to "let off some steam," but that, as a result of this activity, one student suffers an asthma attack. Would it make a difference if the teacher's intent was to develop a better learning environment through more competitive group spirit? Would it matter if the asthma attack occurred after the football coach ordered all the defensive linemen to run around the track five times because of their poor performance in last week's game? What if the coach claims he ordered the laps because he believed the linemen needed to develop increased stamina? How does one distinguish students' improper, remediable behavior from simple lack of talent or inadequacy? Is punishment for one allowable, but not for the other?

Sometimes when school personnel strike children it is absolutely clear that the act is intended as a punishment. A typical scenario would include several components: undesired behavior by the pupil, reprimand and warning by the teacher, repetition of the objectionable behavior, a trip to the principal's office. There, after confirming the circumstances of the misbehavior with the teacher and checking the child's records to determine whether any reason exists *not* to administer corporal punishment (special medical or psychological factors, an Individual Education Plan that precludes corporal punishment, prior parental veto, etc.), the principal obtains a witness and, in the witness's presence, informs the pupil the reason for the punishment and then delivers the swat.

Under such circumstances, there can be little doubt that the striking was intended as punishment. But what of the teacher who "loses his cool" and in a sudden fury slaps a child's face or the exasperated coach who in frustration punches an athlete on the arm? Is this *punishment*, or is it something else, something purely reactive, an almost involuntary, physical lashing out? Between adult strangers, such behavior would surely constitute a battery, but in a school setting it might be permissible, depending upon the precise language of the governing corporal punishment statute.

Definition is critical to the determination of what behaviors will be sanctioned within any particular school setting. Absent clarity of definition, all participants are left to their own individual interpretations, and these are only validated when a particular incident is contested. To confine a definition to a phrase like "striking with a paddle" is clearly too restrictive, yet to broaden it to include any action that "causes distress to the body" risks overinclusiveness. One would hope for a definition broad enough to encompass future actions that are of the same type as those particularized in the statute (e.g., shoving a student into a chalkboard), yet not so general as to include commonplace, acceptable teacher behavior associated with maintaining order in school (e.g., isolating two students after a fight).

At the very least, corporal punishment must be defined in terms of: 1) force that is *physical* and not merely verbal; 2) activity that is intended as *punishment* as differentiated from instructional strategy; 3) the degree of *intent* required; 4) whether *physical deprivation* and *social isolation* are included; 5) the *degree of pain* or distress that provides a definitional threshold. These five considerations are minimally required for a law to be usefully predictive. Other considerations emerge as one begins to focus on operational issues. These are especially illuminated as one examines existing statutes from two perspectives: the *substantive position* taken by each regulation and the *locus of authority* from which it derives its power to determine corporal punishment policy. By asking a number of analytical questions, one begins the process of uncovering how the law in this area works and, ultimately, what the law means to all the various participants in the school community.

Analytical Questions

Because local corporal punishment practice is often governed by policy that has been set at more than one level of government, there can be no universal formula for determining what is permitted or forbidden within any particular district, county or state. Similarly, it is impossible to point to a single law and say, "This is the definitive statute to authorize — or to ban — corporal punishment." Instead, one must ask a series of questions to determine, in any given jurisdiction, what is allowed and what is not. The purpose of such questions is to tease apart the many strands of an interwoven, multi-layered situation. Although these individual components are rarely found in isolation, for analytical purposes it is helpful to examine them separately. And to comprehend the variety of positions that may be assumed *vis-à-vis* these several sub-issues, it is useful to examine excerpts of existing statutes, regulations and local policy statements; these are therefore included following each question. The authors particularly appreciate those school districts that have shared their policy statements in this study. In an attempt to bring some order to an area of inquiry that is otherwise confusing, the defining questions have been organized into three main groups. The first of these relates to questions of *authority and rationale*: where does the authority regulating corporal punishment come from, and what is its stated basis? A second group of questions relates to *procedures governing administration* of corporal punishment: under what conditions may corporal punishment be administered, and what procedural rights might be established for those youngsters upon whom this punishment is inflicted? A final section inquires into the *liabilities* of — and the *protections* afforded to — those school personnel who may have wrongfully administered corporal punishment and whose behavior has been challenged as inappropriate or illegal.

A. LEGAL AUTHORITY AND RATIONALE FOR CORPORAL PUNISHMENT POLICY

1. *Is there a state statute that authorizes, limits or forbids corporal punishment in schools?*

"Corporal punishment shall be prohibited in public schools." (NEB. REV. STAT. §79-4,140)

"Any teacher or school principal may use corporal punishment in a reasonable manner against any pupil for good cause in order to maintain discipline and order within the public schools." (ARK. STAT. ANN. §6-18-505)

It should be noted that, if state statutes are silent, common law within each state may suggest an implied authorization or limitation on the rights of school personnel to administer corporal punishment.

2. **Is there a state statute that delegates the authority to determine corporal punishment policy to a particular agency, level of school administration, or category of educational personnel?**

"The county board of each of the counties listed in paragraph (1) of this subsection may adopt rules and regulations governing the use of corporal punishment." (MD. EDUC. CODE ANN. §7-305 (3))

"A board of education may adopt a rule prohibiting the use of corporal punishment as a means of discipline in the schools of the district." (OHIO REV. CODE ANN. §3313.20)

"An individual school within a district may establish a school discipline policy, provided that parents, school personnel and students are involved in its development and a public hearing is held in the school prior to its adoption." (N.M. STAT. ANN. §22-5-4.3)

"Every teacher and administrator in the public schools of this State shall have the right to exercise the same authority as to control behavior and discipline over any pupil during any school activity as the parents or guardians may exercise over such pupils. The above authority may include corporal punishment where deemed necessary." (DEL. CODE ANN. tit. 14 §701)

3. **Do state education agency regulations affect the administration of corporal punishment? Are these regulations prescriptive or merely advisory?**

"In the absence of state statute forbidding corporal punishment, it is generally agreed by the courts that the teacher may administer corporal punishment. This is not to say, however, that the State Board recommends corporal punishment, in fact, we would recommend that corporal punishment not be used." (Idaho State Board of Education IDAPA 08.02 Appx. I)

"No person employed by or engaged in a public school shall inflict or cause to be inflicted corporal punishment upon a pupil." (CAL. EDUC. CODE §49001 (b))

4. *Do the regulations of other state agencies affect the manner in which educational personnel may engage in corporal punishment or in the manner that suspected abuse is investigated?*

"... [T]he division of family services shall not have jurisdiction over or investigate any report of alleged child abuse arising out of or related to any spanking administered in a reasonable manner by any school personnel pursuant to a written policy of discipline established by the board of education of the school district." (MO. ANN. STAT. §160.261 (5))

5. *Does local school board policy regulate corporal punishment?*

"As a matter of board policy, reasonable corporal punishment of a student is permitted as a disciplinary measure in order to preserve an effective educational environment which is free from disruption and is conducive to furthering the educational mission of the school." (School District of Kershaw County, South Carolina)

"Since corporal punishment is personally demeaning and totally ineffective in the long run, District 9-R chooses not to include its use as a disciplinary tool." (District 9R, Durango, Colorado)

6. *If authority to make corporal punishment policy is delegated from one level or agency to another, are guidelines issued indicating how local decisions are to be made or how collaborative policy-making is to occur?*

"The local board of education shall adopt a policy for the control and discipline of all children attending public school in that district. Such policy shall provide options for the methods of control and discipline of the students and shall define standards of conduct to which the students are expected to conform. In formulation of such policy, the local board of education shall make an effort to involve the teachers, parents and students affected." (OKLA. STAT. ANN. tit. 70 §6-114)

"A board of education may adopt a rule prohibiting the use of corporal punishment as a means of discipline in the schools of the district. Such rule shall not prohibit the use of force or restraint in accordance with division (B) of section 3319.41 of the Revised Code." (OHIO REV. CODE ANN. §3313.20)

"In deciding upon the appropriate method of correction, the teacher, principal, or his designee should consider the following factors: the amount of injury or harm to persons or property caused by the student's misconduct; the degree to which the student's act(s) of misconduct disturbed the school or class; the number of times the student has committed the same or similar acts of misconduct; and the age and maturity of the student." (Winston-Salem/ Forsyth County Schools)

"Local school boards shall establish student discipline policies and shall file them with the department of education. The local school board shall involve parents, school personnel and students in the development of these policies, and public hearings shall be held during the formulation of these policies in the high school attendance areas within each district or on a district-wide basis for those districts which have no high school." (N.M. STAT. ANN. §22-5-4.3A)

7. *In the event of delegation, does the delegating body retain any ongoing control or any means of obtaining feedback?*

"If an individual school adopts a discipline policy in addition to the local school board's district policy, it shall submit its policy to the local school board for approval." (N.M. STAT. ANN. §22-5-4.3)

"The school board shall have its official discipline plan legally audited on an annual basis to assure that its policies and procedures are currently in compliance with applicable statutes, case law and state and federal constitutional provisions." (MISS. CODE ANN. §37-11-53)

8. *Do the rules on corporal punishment relate to other regulations and if so, is the relationship between them made clear?*

"No local board of education shall promulgate or continue in effect a rule, regulation or bylaw which prohibits the use of such force as is specified in this section." (N.C. GEN. STAT. §115C-390)

"Every resolution, bylaw, rule, ordinance, or other act or authority permitting or authorizing corporal punishment to be inflicted upon a pupil attending a school or educational institution shall be void." (N.J. STAT. ANN. §18A:6-1)

"Spanking, when administered by certified personnel of a school district in a reasonable manner in accordance with the local board of education's written policy of discipline, is not abuse within the meaning of chapter 210 RSMo." (MO. ANN. STAT. §160.261)

"In any case in which the punishment is excessive, such pupil [in a penal or reformatory institution] shall have the same civil and criminal remedies as any other pupil in the public schools." (TENN. CODE ANN. §49-6-4404)

9. *In what terms is corporal punishment described? Which behaviors or activities are included and which are specifically excluded?*

"Corporal punishment is defined as the infliction of physical pain for the purpose of punishment." (Wenatchee School District 246, Washington)

"For the purpose of this chapter, corporal punishment means the intentional infliction of physical pain upon the body of a pupil as a disciplinary measure." (VT. STAT. ANN. tit. 16 §1161a)

"Corporal punishment shall refer to the use of an open hand, paddle, switch, or like instrument on the buttocks." (School District #1, Johnson Co. Wyoming)

"Corporal punishment is defined as the infliction of bodily pain as a penalty for disapproved behavior. However, in the definition of corporal punishment it is necessary to include under the phrase 'infliction of bodily pain' not only striking, but any action which seeks to induce bodily pain, for example, forcing the student to stand on tip toes with finger-tips outstretched against the wall, or to crouch or bend over and remain in such painful cramped positions for long periods of time, or to run laps around the building or in the gym until exhausted, etc." (Southfield, Michigan School Board)

"This definition shall not include physical pain or discomfort caused by participation in practice or competition in an interscholastic sport, or participation in physical education or an extracurricular activity." (VA. CODE ANN. §22.1-279.1)

"For the purpose of this section, "corporal punishment" means conduct involving: (1) hitting or spanking a person with or without an object; or (2) unreasonable physical force that causes bodily harm or substantial emotional harm." (MINN. STAT. ch. 127.45)

10. *Exactly who is authorized to make a paddling decision? Does the decision of one person require ratification by another?*

"Superintendents, principals, supervisors, and teachers shall have authority, to administer such physical punishment on an insubordinate or disobedient student that is reasonable and necessary for supervisory control over the student. Like authority over students is given any person delegated to supervise children who have been authorized to attend a school function away from their school premises and to school bus drivers while students are riding, boarding, or leaving the buses." (S.D. CODIFIED LAWS ANN. §13-32-2)

"The final decision to administer corporal punishment rests with the school principal." (Darlington County School District, South Carolina)

"The principal shall determine which students shall be exempt from paddling due to medical or psychological reasons." (Muskogee Public Schools, Oklahoma)

"If it appears that reasonable corporal punishment is likely to become necessary, the teacher should confer with the principal and the principal and teacher should be in agreement on the necessity of corporal punishment." (Pitt County Board of Education, North Carolina)

"The employee who is to administer corporal punishment and the employee, if any, who initiated the disciplinary measures which are to result in the administration of corporal punishment must confer and they must agree on the necessity for corporal punishment in each instance." (Bibb County Public Schools, Georgia)

"The use of corporal punishment shall be approved in principle by the principal before it is used, but approval is not necessary for each specific instance in which it is used." (FLA. STAT. ANN. §232.27)

11. *To what extent is the authority to administer corporal punishment determined by time of day or locale?*

"Every teacher is authorized to hold every pupil strictly accountable for any disorderly conduct in school or on the playground of the school, or on any school bus going to or returning from school, or during intermission or recess." (ARK. STAT. ANN. §6-18-505)

"Every teacher, vice principal and principal in the public schools shall have the right to exercise the same authority as to conduct and behavior over the pupils attending his school, during the time they are in attendance, including the time required in going to and from their homes, as the parents, guardians or persons in parental relation to such pupils may exercise over them." (24 PA. CONS. STAT. ANN. §13-1317)

"The teacher shall . . . have control of all pupils enrolled in the school from the time they reach the school until they have returned to their respective homes, except that where transportation of pupils is provided, the driver in charge of the school bus or other mode of transportation shall exercise such authority and control over the children while they are in transit...." (W. Va. CODE §18A-5-1)

12. *Precisely who is authorized to administer corporal punishment, and who is not? Does the regulation impose any obligation or liability upon a bystander or witness to impermissible corporal punishment?*

"Where corporal punishment is deemed necessary, it may be administered by any public school teacher or administrator in accordance with district board of education policy." (DEL. CODE ANN. tit. 14 §701)

"Corporal punishment is permitted by supervisors but not by teachers." (Orangeburg County School District No. 5, South Carolina)

"A person employed by or engaged as a volunteer or contractor by a local or intermediate school board shall not threaten to inflict, inflict, or cause to be inflicted corporal punishment upon any pupil." (MICH. COMP. LAWS ANN. §380.1312 (2))

13. *Which students are susceptible to corporal punishment? Is any particular group included or excluded? Are certain types of schools covered and not others? Does the scope of the authorization or limitation include private schools, reform schools, schools for the severely handicapped, religious schools, and day care centers?*

"No teacher, principal or other person employed by a school board or employed in a school operated by the Commonwealth shall subject a student to corporal punishment." (VA. CODE ANN. §22.1-279.1)

"No person employed or engaged in a school or educational institution, whether public or private, shall inflict or cause to be inflicted corporal punishment upon a pupil attending such school or institution...." (N.J. STAT. ANN §18A:6-1

"Corporal punishment shall not be administered to a pupil: (a) Identified as handicapped, learning, hearing mentally or behaviorally disabled; or (b) whose parent has petitioned in writing to the school principal that corporal punishment not be administered to the pupil and attached a certificate from a physician that by reason of a physical or emotional condition the pupil should not be subjected to corporal punishment; or (c) if medical information available to school authorities indicates that the pupil should not be subjected to corporal punishment." (W. VA. CODE §18A-5-1(10))

"For the special education student, provision for the use of corporal punishment shall be in accordance with the student's IEP [Individual Education Plan]" (New Castle, Delaware)

"Corporal punishment should never be administered to a child whom school personnel know to be under psychological or physical treatment without a conference with the psychologist or physician." (Lincoln Public Schools, Illinois)

"Corporal punishment is a serious yet, at times appropriate disciplinary measure for students in kindergarten through junior high." (New Castle, Delaware)

14. *Does the regulation specify particular pupil behaviors that corporal punishment may be used to punish?*

"In the absence of any statute or rule or regulation of the board of trustees, any teacher employed by a school district shall have the right to direct how and when each pupil shall attend to his appropriate duties, and the manner in which a pupil shall demean himself while in attendance at the school." (IDAHO CODE §33-1224)

"List of Acts which may Result in Corporal Punishment
—**Acts Shocking to the Conscience**. Examples: Stealing;
Cheating; Vulgarity, Profanity, Possession of Pornography;
Intimidation; Urinating on Others; Deliberate Destruction
of Property; Acts which can cause Bodily Harm to other
Students or Staff." (Pitt County, North Carolina)

"Corporal punishment is available for the following
offenses: abusive language, extortion, general school/class-
room disruption, inflammatory actions, loitering, offensive
touching." (New Castle, Delaware)

**15. *Does the formal authorization or limitation of cor-
poral punishment include a clear rationale for the
position taken?***

"It is the policy of this state to protect children from
assault and abuse and to encourage parents, teachers, and
their authorized agents to use methods of correction and
restraint of children that are not dangerous to the children.
However, the physical discipline of a child is not unlawful
when it is reasonable and moderate and is inflicted by a parent, teacher or guardian for the purposes of restraining or
correcting the child." (WASH. REV. CODE ANN. §9A.16.100)

"Parents should be the first to foster self-discipline within the child at home; and even though the ultimate aim for
each child is self-discipline, the Board of Education feels
that enforcement and support of the authority of our
teachers and principals are essential as children are led to
the point of disciplining themselves." (Claremore City
Schools, Oklahoma)

"As a matter of board policy, reasonable corporal punishment of a student is permitted as a disciplinary measure
in order to preserve an effective educational environment
which is free from disruption and is conducive to furthering the educational mission of the board." (School District of Kershaw County, South Carolina)

"The right to procedural due process also includes the right to receive a punishment which fits the wrong done by the student." (Winston-Salem/Forsyth County Schools, North Carolina)

"The legislature finds and declares that the protection against corporal punishment, which extends to other citizens in other walks of life, should include children when they are under the control of the public schools. Children of school age are at the most vulnerable and impressionable period of their lives and it is wholly reasonable that the safeguards to the integrity and sanctity of their bodies should be, at this tender age, at least equal to that afforded to other citizens." (CAL. EDUC. CODE §49000)

"Corporal punishment is a serious yet, at times, appropriate disciplinary measure for students in kindergarten through junior high." (New Castle, Delaware)

"Teachers...are not granted authority to use force in order to punish....It is necessary for a teacher to have order so that he may teach, and subsection 2 gives him authority to maintain order when a child is creating a disturbance...." (Comment to ME. REV. STAT. ANN. tit. 17A §106)

"Each student shall have the right to respect from teachers, other students, administrators, and other school personnel, and shall not be subject to ridicule, harassment, or any punishment that is demeaning or derogatory. No student shall be subject to corporal punishment." (D.C. Municipal Regulations tit. 5 §2401.12)

16. *Has the state enacted "in loco parentis" legislation specifically granting parental-like authority to teachers and principals?*

"...[The] teacher of a child attending a public school shall have the same right as a parent or guardian to control and discipline such child according to local policies during the time the child is in attendance or in transit to or from the school or any other school function authorized by the

school district or classroom presided over by the teacher."
(OKLA. STAT. ANN. tit. 70 §6-114)

"In all matters relating to the discipline in and conduct
of the schools and the school children, [educational per-
sonnel] stand in the relation of parents and guardians to
the pupils...." (ILL. REV. STAT. ch. 122, para. 34-84a)

17. *What general duties are ascribed to teachers and
administrators that provide a rationale for their specific authority to paddle students?*

"Every teacher shall seek to exercise wholesome discipline... and endeavor by precept and otherwise to instill
and cultivate in the pupils good morals and gentle man-
ners." (ARK. STAT. ANN. §6-18-501)

"Each school principal shall be responsible for the
maintenance of discipline in his school." (W. VA. CODE
§18A-5-1 (9))

"Every teacher shall: (4) hold pupils to strict account
for disorderly conduct." (ARIZ. REV. STAT. ANN. §15-521)

"...[A] teacher shall have the power to adopt any reasonable rule or regulation to control and maintain discipline in, and otherwise govern, the classroom, not incon-
sistent with any statute or rule or regulation of the board
of trustees." (IDAHO CODE §33-1224)

18. *Does the state have a general "justification of force"
statute that applies to school personnel?*

"The use of physical force upon another person which
would otherwise constitute an offence is justifiable and not
criminal under any of the following circumstances: (1)...
[A] teacher or other person entrusted with the care and
supervision of a person under the age of twenty-one for a
special purpose, may use physical force, but not deadly
physical force, upon such person when and to the extent

that he reasonably believes it necessary to maintain discipline or to promote the welfare of such person." (N.Y. PENAL LAW §35.10)

"Any person employed by the district may, within the scope of his employment, use reasonable and appropriate physical intervention or force as necessary for the following purposes: (1) To restrain a student from an act of wrong-doing; (2) To quell a disturbance threatening physical injury to others; (3) To obtain possession of weapons or other dangerous objects upon a student or within the control of a student; (4) For the purpose of self-defence; (5) For the protection of persons or property; (6) For the preservation of order." (Cripple Creek-Victor School District, Colorado)

"A person to whom such parent, foster parent, guardian or other responsible person has expressly delegated permission to so prevent or punish misconduct is similarly justified in using a reasonable degree of force." (ME. REV. STAT. ANN. tit. 17-A §106 (1))

19. *Does the statute, rule, or regulation impose a duty on supervisors to be responsible for any corporal punishment administered by their subordinates?*

"No teacher, administrator, student or other person shall subject a student to corporal punishment or condone the use of corporal punishment by any person under his or her supervision or control." (D.C. Municipal Regulations tit. 5 §2403)

"Any superintendent of schools, president of a school board or his designee, or juvenile officer who knowingly falsifies any report of any matter pursuant to this section or who knowingly withholds any information relative to any investigation or report pursuant to this section is guilty of a class A misdemeanor." (MO. STAT. ANN. §160.261 (7))

20. ***What general duties have been ascribed to pupils, the breach of which might be used to impose subsequent punishment?***

"Public school pupils shall comply with rules for the government of such schools, pursue the prescribed course of study, use the prescribed textbooks and submit to the teachers' authority." (OR. REV. STAT. ANN. §339.250)

"Any pupil who continually and willfully disobeys the provisions of this section, shows open defiance of the authority vested in school personnel by this section, defaces or damages any school building, school grounds, furniture, equipment, book belonging to the district, or harms or threatens to harm another person or his property shall be liable for punishment, suspension, or expulsion under the provisions of this title...." (MONT. CODE ANN. §20-5-201)

B. ISSUES INVOLVING THE ACTUAL PROCEDURES EMPLOYED DURING ADMINISTRATION OF CORPORAL PUNISHMENT

21. ***Are limits imposed on where the swat may be placed?***

"No part of the body above the waist or below the knees may be struck." (Bibb County Public Schools, Georgia)

"No corporal punishment may be administered on or about the head or face of any pupil, but this limitation does not prohibit any teacher, principal or other licensed person from defending himself if attacked by a pupil." (NEV. REV. STAT. ANN. §392.465 (4))

"Not about the face or head" (Forsyth County Schools, North Carolina)

22. ***Are limits imposed on how many times an offender may be struck?***

"[In] the primary grades, classroom teachers may administer corporal punishment occasionally where beneficial to the child involved. In all such cases only the hand may be used to spank the child once on the buttock." (Lincoln Public Schools, Illinois)

"If it is determined that the student has misbehaved and that corporal punishment is necessary, the principal or a designee must determine how many licks and under what circumstance they will be administered." (LaGrange School System, Georgia)

"A limit of one to three swats for any one incident" (Claremore City Schools, Oklahoma)

"Avoid excessive corporal punishment. Accumulation of swats in a short period, such as a school day, can cause severe bruising of the child." (Muskogee Public Schools, Oklahoma)

23. *What instruments, if any, are permitted? Are certain techniques favored or prohibited?*

"...nothing contained in this act shall prohibit any parent, teacher or other person from using ordinary force as a means of discipline, including but not limited to spanking, switching or paddling." (OKLA. STAT. ANN. tit. 21 §844)

"The instrument used to administer corporal punishment shall be the standard paddle approved by the District." (Orangeburg County School District No. 5, South Carolina)

"No cruel or unusual form of corporal punishment shall be inflicted upon any student, including but not limited to restraint by binding arms, legs, or torso, washing out the mouth with soap, and verbal abuse." (Yakima Public Schools, Washington)

"There will only be one paddle in each school; it shall be located in the principal's office. It shall be 24" by 5" by 3/8"." (Caddo Parish, Louisiana)

24. *Are any limitations placed on the severity of the swat?*

"Pupils may not be stricken on or about the head in any way, or in any manner be subjected to any brutal or unreasonable punishment." (CODE OF MD. Regulations tit. 13A §08.01.06 (B))

"No person shall . . . [a]dminister corporal punishment or other physical disciplinary measure, or physically restrain the child in a cruel manner or for a prolonged period, which punishment, discipline, or restraint is excessive under the circumstances and creates a substantial risk of serious physical harm to the child." (OHIO REV. CODE ANN. 2919.22 (B)(3))

"Effort should be made not to injure or bruise the child." (Claremore City Schools, Oklahoma)

"The following actions are presumed unreasonable when used to correct or restrain a child: (1) Throwing, kicking, burning, or cutting a child; (2) striking a child with a closed fist; (3) shaking a child under age three; (4) interfering with a child's breathing; (5) threatening a child with a deadly weapon; or (6) doing any other act that is likely to cause and which does cause bodily harm greater than transient pain or minor temporary marks. The age, size, and condition of the child and the location of the injury shall be considered when determining whether bodily harm is reasonable or moderate. This list is illustrative of unreasonable actions and is not intended to be exclusive." (WASH. REV. CODE ANN. §9A.16.100)

25. *Are additional conditions imposed by the regulations that govern how corporal punishment is to be administered?*

"Punishment is administered without anger or malice. The amount of physical force used is not wanton or in excess of the offense, is suitable to the pupil's age and mental and physical conditions and is applied without discrimination." (W. VA. CODE §18A-5-1)

"To be effective, corporal punishment must be administered soon after the violation for which it is given." (Colonial School District, Delaware)

"Students shall not be required to remove clothing when being punished." (Pennsylvania Administrative Regulations §12.5 (e))

26. *Are certain attitudes, motives, or states of mind on the part of the punisher proscribed?*

"Corporal punishment...shall be administered in kindness and at a time and under conditions not calculated to hold the child up to ridicule or shame." (Macon, Georgia)

"It shall be unlawful...to intimidate, threaten or coerce...any person enrolled in any school...." (MISS. CODE ANN. §37-11-20)

"If such punishment is required, it shall be administered with extreme care, tact and caution...." (Monroe City Schools, Louisiana)

"Punishment [shall be] administered without anger or malice." (W. VA. CODE §18A-5-1 (4))

"Care should be exercised by the person administering the corporal punishment that (s)he is not emotionally upset at the time." (Silver Consolidated Schools, New Mexico)

27. *Is any special setting required where the punishment is to be administered?*

"Corporal punishment shall not be administered in a classroom with other children present." (N.C. GEN. STAT. §115C-391 (a) (1))

"Corporal punishment shall not be administered in front of other students or in such ways as to humiliate a pupil in front of his/her peers." (Asheville City Schools, North Carolina)

28. *Is a particular witness required to be present?*

"A teacher or principal may administer corporal punishment only in the presence of another adult who is informed beforehand, and in the student's presence, of the reason for the punishment." (FLA. STAT. ANN. §232.27 (3))

"Only a teacher, substitute teacher, principal, or assistant principal may administer corporal punishment and may do so only in the presence of a principal, assistant principal, teacher, substitute teacher, teacher aide or assistant or student teacher, who shall be informed beforehand and in the student's presence of the reason for the punishment" (N.C. GEN. STAT. §115C-391)

"A female professional shall be present if corporal punishment is administered to a female student." (Caddo Parish, Louisiana)

29. *Are limitations placed on when corporal punishment may be employed, in relation to other forms of discipline?*

"Corporal punishment should be administered only as a last resort after use of alternative methods of discipline have failed to correct the inappropriate pupil behavior" (W. VA. CODE §18A-5-1)

"Except for those acts of misconduct which are extremely anti-social or disruptive in nature, corporal punishment should never be used unless the student is informed beforehand that specific behavior could occasion its use; and, subject to this exception, it should never be used as a first line of punishment." (Monroe City Schools, Louisiana)

"Corporal punishment should be regarded as a last resort and may be employed only in cases where other means in seeking cooperation from the students have failed.... [C]orporal punishment should not be a used as a first line of punishment for misbehavior except for response to those actions which are listed in "I" as "acts of misconduct which are so antisocial or disruptive in nature as to shock the conscience." Actions which could result in corporal punishment are listed under "II." A further refinement and definition of those acts should be made by each school and published annually in faculty and student handbooks." (Pitt County Board of Education, North Carolina)

30. *What advance notice, if any, is required for the child?*

"The student body shall be informed beforehand what general types of misconduct could result in corporal punishment" (N.C. GEN. STAT. §115C-391)

"The students, teachers, and parents or guardian of every child residing within a school district shall be notified by the local board of education of its adoption of the policy and shall receive a copy upon request." (OKLA. STAT. ANN. tit. 70 §6-114)

31. *What advance notice, if any, is required to be given the parent or guardian? Is it a general notice, listing proscribed behavior punishable by corporal punishment, or is it a specific notice of impending punishment?*

"Parents and guardians must be notified before, or as soon as possible after, corporal punishment is administered" (NEV. REV. STAT. ANN. §392.465 (3))

"If corporal punishment is to be used by school districts as a penalty for misbehavior, the district shall notify parents upon initial enrollment of the student that they may submit a written request that corporal punishment not be administered to their child or children." (Ilinois State Board of Education Doc. No. 1 (1977))

"A report which includes a description of the pupil's conduct prompting the use of corporal punishment and the name of the witness is attempted to be made informally by telephone or notice sent with the child to the parent or guardian at least twelve hours prior to the administration of corporal punishment and is made orally in the school office by the end of the school day and a written report is filed in the school office within twenty-four hours of the incident." (W. VA. CODE §18A-5-1)

"Corporal punishment shall be administered to a student only after the principal of the school has provided written notification to the parents or guardians of the student that the school seeks to administer corporal punishment. Written notification shall be required for each incident in which corporal punishment is the selected form of discipline." (Arizona Department of Education Proposed Rule R7-2-807)

32. *Is a parent given the right to limit the school's use of corporal punishment?*

"At the beginning of each school year, the principal of the school shall send home with each student a consent form for parents or guardians to sign stating whether they want their child to receive corporal punishment." (Orangeburg County, South Carolina)

"Corporal Punishment shall not be administered to a child whose parents or legal guardian has upon the day of enrollment of the pupil filed with the principal of the school a statement from a medical doctor licensed in Georgia stating that it is detrimental to the child's mental or emotional stability." (GA. CODE ANN. §20-2-731 (5))

33. *What type of post-punishment documentation is required? To which individuals or agencies must the required report be forwarded?*

"Each act of corporal punishment shall be documented and reported to the governing board by the district superintendent at least quarterly. Reports shall be maintained in the office of the district superintendent for a period of not less than three years and shall be forwarded to the Department of Education upon request." (ARIZ. REV. STAT. ANN. §15-550)

"A teacher or principal who has administered punishment shall, upon request, provide the pupil's parent or guardian with a written explanation of the reason for the punishment and the name of the other adult who was present." (FLA. STAT. ANN. §232.27 (3))

"The parent or guardian of the pupil is notified in writing of each instance of corporal punishment within three school days." (W. VA. CODE §18A-5-1 (7),(8))

34. Has a review or appeals process been established? Does this become activated before or after the punishment is carried out?

"In cases where a student protests innocence of the offense or ignorance of the rule, a brief but adequate opportunity shall be provided for the student to explain his side of the situation." (Monroe City Schools, Louisiana)

"A discipline committee may be formed in each school for the purpose of reviewing each case brought before it and recommending to the principal the necessary action to be taken. The committee shall consist of five teachers assigned by the principal with one member assigned by him as chairman.... The committee shall function as a body in the following manner: (1) Act only upon cases presented to it by the principal; (2) Review written report from principal; (3) Provide hearing for pupil and parents as advisable; (4) Evaluate the incident, the past history, and the statements and conduct of the pupil during the hearing; and (5) Make thorough written report and recommendations to the principal. All recommendations shall be made by consent of the simple majority of those present at the hearing. (Grand County School District, Utah)

C. CONSEQUENCES TO THE PUNISHER: LIABILITIES AND PROTECTUIONS

35. *Does the statute itself mandate a punishment or a punishment process for those who may violate its provisions?*

"A person who violates subsection (2) may be appropriately disciplined by his or her school board." (MICH. COMP. LAWS ANN. §380.1312)

"Any superintendent of schools, president of a school board or his designee, or juvenile officer who knowingly falsifies any report of any matter pursuant to this section or who knowingly withholds any information relative to any investigation or report pursuant to this section is guilty of a class A misdemeanor." (MO. ANN. STAT. §160.261 (7))

36. *Are local school districts required to develop procedures for disciplining teachers who have violated the rules governing corporal punishment?*

"The governing board shall: (25) Prescribe and enforce rules for disciplinary action against a teacher who engages in conduct which is in violation of the rules or policies of the governing board but which is not cause for dismissal of the teacher or for revocation of the certificate of the teacher." (ARIZ. REV. STAT. ANN. §15-341)

37. *Does a finding of improper administration of corporal punishment affect a teacher's right to hold a teaching certificate?*

"Evidence that a person has injured the health or welfare of a child through physical or sexual abuse or exploitation shall be grounds for revocation or suspension of a certificate." (ME. REV. STAT. tit 20A §13020 (2) (A))

38. *Does the statute create a civil cause of action against violators? Does it specify the nature of allowable evidence?*

"Except as provided in s. 939.61 (1), this section does not create a separate basis for civil liability of a school board or their official employees or agents for damages arising out of claims involving allegations of improper or unnecessary use of force by school employees against students." (WIS. STAT. ANN. §118.31)

"If a teacher or any other person acting in good faith and in compliance with the discipline code adopted by the board of education pursuant to subsection (2) of this section shall be immune from civil liability; except that a person acting willfully or wantonly shall not be immune from liability pursuant to this subparagraph (II). The court shall dismiss any civil action resulting from actions taken by a teacher or any other person pursuant to the discipline code upon a finding by the court that the person acted in good faith and in compliance with such discipline code and was therefore immune from civil liability pursuant to this subparagraph (II)." (COLO. REV. STAT. §22-32-110)

"The principal or teacher who administered corporal punishment must provide the child's parent, upon request, a written explanation of the reasons for the punishment and the name of the principal or assistant or designee of the principal or assistant principal, who was present; provided, however, that such an explanation shall not be used as evidence in any subsequent civil action brought as a result of the corporal punishment." (GA. CODE ANN. §20-2-731)

39. *Does the statute create a criminal action against violators?*

"If a person who is employed or engaged by a school district uses corporal punishment or more physical restraint than reasonable or necessary, the person is guilty of a misdemeanor and, upon conviction of the misdemeanor by a court of competent jurisdiction, shall be fined not less than $25 or more than $500." (MONT. CODE ANN. §20-4-302)

"Whoever violates this section is guilty of endangering children. If the offender violates division (A) or (B)(1) of this section, endangering children is a misdemeanor of the first degree, except that if a violation results in serious harm to the child involved, or if the offender has previously been convicted of an offense under this section or of any offense involving neglect, abandonment, contribution to the delinquency of, or physical abuse of a child, endangering children is a felony of the fourth degree. If the offender violates division (B)(2), (3), or (4) of this section, endangering children is a felony of the third degree, except that if the violation results in serious harm to the child involved, or if the offender has previously been convicted of an offense under this section or of any offense involving neglect, abandonment, contributing to the delinquency of, or physical abuse of a child, endangering children is a felony of the second degree...." (OHIO REV. CODE ANN. §2919.22)

40. *Does the statute immunize school employees facing civil action?*

"Each school committee and the board of regents shall protect and save harmless any public school teacher, or any supervisor or administrator or other employee thereof whose position requires a certificate from the department of education or board of regents for elementary and secondary education from financial loss and expense, including legal fees and costs, if any, arising out of any claim, demand or suit for actions resulting in accidental bodily injury to or death of any person, or in accidental damage to or destruction of property, within or without the school building, or other acts, including but not limited to infringement of any person's civil rights, resulting in any injury, when acts are not wanton, reckless, malicious, or grossly negligent, as determined by a court of competent jurisdiction, provided such teacher, supervisor, or administrator, at the time of the acts resulting in such injury, death, damages or destruction was acting in the discharge of his or her duties or within the scope of his or her employment or under the direction of such school committee or the board of regents." (R.I. GEN. LAWS §9-1-31)

"No school employee who in good faith reports any known or suspected violation of the school discipline poli-

cy or in good faith attempts to enforce the policy shall be
held liable for any civil damages as a result of such report
or of his efforts to enforce any part of the policy." (N.M.
STAT. ANN. §22-5-4.3)

41. *Does the statute protect teachers or others from retribution by the school system itself?*

"A teacher or any person who acts in good faith and in
compliance with the discipline code adopted by the board
of education pursuant to subsection (2) of this section
shall not have his contract nonrenewed or be subject to
any disciplinary proceedings, including dismissal, as a
result of such lawful actions, nor shall the actions of such
person be reflected in any written evaluation or other personnel record concerning such person." (COLO. REV.
STAT. §22-32-110)

42. *Does the statute establish immunity for teachers accused of criminal violations?*

"No action taken by a teacher or principal pursuant to
the provision of this part shall be grounds for the issuance
of an arrest warrant or for the pressing of criminal charges
against such teacher or principal unless a report of an
investigation by appropriate law enforcement officials
along with independent medical verification of injury is
presented to the judge or magistrate prior to issuing such a
warrant. The investigative findings shall be presented to
the judge or magistrate within fifteen (15) days of receipt
of notification. The law enforcement agency shall give
notice to the superintendent of schools or his designee at
the time it is notified of the allegations." (TENN. CODE
ANN. §49-6-4103)

"Except in the case of excessive force or cruel and
unusual punishment, a teacher or other member of the
instructional staff, a principal or his designated representative, or a bus driver shall not be civilly or criminally liable
for any action carried out in conformity with the state
board and district school board rules regarding the control, suspension, and expulsion of students." (FLA. STAT.
ANN. §232.275)

43. Does the statute create an affirmative defense for those accused of wrongdoing?

"A person named as a defendant in an action brought under this section may assert as an affirmative defense that the use of physical restraint was reasonable or necessary. If that defense is denied by the person bringing the charge, the issue of whether the restraint used was reasonable or necessary must be determined by the trier of fact." (MONT. CODE ANN. §20-4-302)

"If a criminal action is brought against a teacher or any other person, it shall be an affirmative defense in such criminal action that the teacher or such other person was acting in good faith and in compliance with the discipline code adopted by the board of education pursuant to subsection (2) of this section and was not acting in a willful or wanton manner." (COLO. REV. STAT. §22-32-110)

44. Does the statute give specific guidance to judges and juries weighing possible wrongdoing?

"In determining whether or not a person was acting within the exceptions to sub. (3), deference shall be given to reasonable, good faith judgments made by an official, employee or agent of a school board." (WIS. STAT. ANN. §118.31)

"In determining whether a person was acting within the exceptions provided in this section, due deference shall be given to reasonable judgments at the time of the event which were made by a teacher, principal or other person employed by a school board or employed in a school operated by the Commonwealth." (VA. CODE ANN. §22.1-279.1)

45. Does immunization provide payment of court costs and attorney's fees? Are conditions attached?

"Each board of education shall protect and save harmless...any teacher...from financial loss and expense...arising out of any claim...by reason of alleged negligence ...including...infringement of any person's civil rights...

which acts are not wanton, reckless or malicious, providing such teacher...was acting...within the scope of employment." (CONN. GEN. STAT. §10-235 (a))

"The court shall award court costs and reasonable attorney fees to the prevailing party in such a civil action." (COLO. REV. STAT. §22-32-110)

"Should any teacher, principal, or administrator in the public school system be sued for damages by any student, the parent of any student or other persons qualified to bring suit on behalf of such student based upon the act or omission of such teacher, principal, or administrator in the directing of and disciplining of school children under their care and supervision it shall be the responsibility of the school board employing such teacher, principal, or administrator to provide such defendant with a legal defense to such suit including reasonable attorney's fees, investigatory costs, and other related expenses. Should any such teacher, principal, or administrator be cast in judgment for damages in such suit, it shall be the obligation of the school board employing such defendant to indemnify him fully against such judgment including all principal, interest, and costs. Nothing in this Section shall require a school board to indemnify a teacher, principal, or administrator against a judgment wherein there is a specific decree in the judgment that the action of the teacher, principal, or administrator was malicious, and willfully and deliberately intended to cause bodily harm." (LA. REV. STAT. ANN. tit. 17 §416.1)

46. Has a grievance procedure been established for parents or for children claiming wrongful punishment?

"On or before January 1, 1989, each city and parish school board shall adopt a policy establishing procedures for the investigation of employees accused of impermissible corporal punishment or moral offenses involving students." (LA. REV. STAT. ANN. tit. 17 §81.6)

"Any student, parent, or guardian who is aggrieved by the imposition of discipline shall have the right to an informal conference with the building principal or his or her designee for the purpose of resolving the grievance. The employee whose action is being grieved shall be notified of the initiation of a grievance as soon as reasonably possible. During such conference the student, parent, or guardian shall be subject to questioning by the building principal or his or her designee and shall be entitled to question school personnel involved in the matter being grieved. Subsequent to the building level grievance meeting, the student, parent, or guardian, upon two school business days' prior notice, shall have the right to present a written and/or oral grievance to the superintendent of the district or his/her designee. If the grievance is not resolved the student, parent, or guardian, upon two school business days' prior notice, shall have the right to present a written and/or oral grievance to the board of directors during the board's next regular meeting. The board shall notify the student, parent, or guardian of its response to the grievance within ten school business days after the date of the meeting. The discipline action shall continue notwithstanding the implementation of the grievance procedure set forth in this section unless the principal or his or her designee elects to postpone such action." (WASH. ADMIN. CODE §180-40-240)

"The provisions of §210.110 to 210.165, RSMo. notwithstanding, the division of family services shall not have jurisdiction over or investigate any report of alleged child abuse arising out of or related to any spanking administered in a reasonable manner by any certificated school personnel pursuant to a written policy of discipline established by the board of education of the school district." (MO. ANN. STAT. 160.261)

"In instances where allegations of abuse of a student are reported against an employee, principal or other school official, through the administering of impermissible corporal punishment or any other moral offense, the Superintendent shall promptly investigate the action." (West Feliciana Parish, Louisiana)

"When an arrest warrant has been issued against a teacher for action taken pursuant to the provisions of this part, then the teacher shall be summoned to an administrative office or to a location other than on school grounds, so that students shall not be present, and shall be arrested there. The teacher is not to be arrested in the classroom or before any assembly of students. Provided, this subsection shall not apply if a law enforcement officer reasonably believes that the teacher will flee from arrest or attempt to leave the jurisdiction of the court which issued the warrant." (TENN. CODE ANN. §49-6-4105)

Conclusion

These questions are illustrative of an approach that attempts to "unpack" each statute, regulation, or policy statement into its constituent parts in such a manner as to encourage further analysis of potential issues and sub-issues, as well as to encourage the generation of new and ever more refined questions. Though neither inclusive nor entirely comprehensive, these questions provide a rudimentary framework for the detailed examination of corporal punishment law. This Section concludes with a compilation of statutes, arranged alphabetically by state, plus a listing of pertinent corporal punishment cases that have arisen at the state level.

STATE STATUTES AND SELECTED CASES

ALABAMA

ALA. CODE § 13A-3-24 (1990) Use of Force by Persons with Parental, Custodial or Special Responsibilities.

State Tenure Comm'n v. Birmingham Bd. of Educ., 555 So. 2d 1068 (Ala. Civ. App. 1989).

Ex parte Alabama State Tenure Comm'n, 555 So. 2d 1071 (Ala. 1989), *reh'g denied*, 1989.

Adams v. City of Dothan Bd. of Educ., 485 So. 2d 757 (Ala. Ct. Civ. App. 1986).

Suits v. Glover, 71 So. 2d 49 (Ala. 1954).

Boyd v. State, 7 So. 2d 268 (Ala. 1889).

ALASKA

ALASKA ADMIN. CODE tit. 4 § 07.010 Establishment of District Guidelines and Procedures. Prohibited discipline.

ALASKA ADMIN. CODE tit. 4 § 07.900 Definition.

ALASKA STAT. § 11.81.430 (1990) Justification: Use of force, special relationships.

Op. Att'y Gen. (Jan. 30, 1986).

Roberts v. Santa Cruz Unified Sch. Dist. No. 35, 778 P.2d 1294 (Ariz. Ct. App. 1989).

Fulton v. Dysart Unified Sch. Dist., 651 P.2d 368 (Ariz. Ct. App. 1982).

ARIZONA

ARIZ. REV. STAT. ANN. § 15-843 (1990) Pupil Disciplinary Proceedings.

ARIZ. REV. STAT. ANN. § 15-341 Duties of Teachers.

ARIZ. REV. STAT. ANN. § 15-521.

ARIZ. REV. STAT. ANN. § 15-550 Failure to Comply with Statutes as Unprofessional Conduct; Penalty.

R7-2-807 (Proposed) Corporal Punishment Guidelines.

Roberts v. Santa Cruz Valley Unified Sch. Dist., 778 P.2d 1294 (Ariz. Ct. App. 1989).

LaFrents v. Gallagher, 462 P.2d 804 (Ariz. 1969).

State v. Hunt, 406 P.2d 208 (Ariz. Ct. App. 1965).

ARKANSAS

ARK. STAT. ANN. § 6-18-501 Teacher's Duty.

ARK. STAT. ANN. § 6-18-505 School Discipline Act.

ARK. STAT. ANN. § 6-18-502 Guidelines for Development of School District Student Discipline Policies.

ARK. STAT. ANN. § 6-18-503 Written Student Discipline Policies Required.

ARK. STAT. ANN. § 6-18-504 Compliance with §§ 6-18-502 and 6-18-503.

ARK. STAT. ANN. § 6-17-1113 Civil liability insurance.

Department of Human Servs. v. Caldwell, 832 S.W.2d 510 (Ark. Ct. App. 1992).

Berry v. Arnold Sch. Dist., 137 S.W.2d 256 (Ark. 1940).

Dodd v. State, 26 S.W. 834 (Ark. 1910).

CALIFORNIA

CAL. EDUC. CODE § 49000 (West 1991).

CAL. EDUC. CODE § 49001 (West 1991).

Letter from Deputy Attorney General Harlan Van Wye to Jordan Riak (1988).

Crowl v. San Juan Unified Sch. Dist., 275 Cal. Rptr. 86 (Cal. Ct. App. 1990).

Slayton v. Pomona Unified Sch. Dist., 207 Cal. Rptr. 705 (Cal. Ct. App. 1984).

Coates v. Cloverdale Unified Sch. Dist. Governing Bd., No. 80029 (Cal. Super. Ct., Sonoma County, January 20, 1975) (Clearinghouse No. 14,462).

People v. Curtis, 300 P. 801 (Cal. Ct. App. 1931).

COLORADO

COLO. REV. STAT. § 22-32-110 (1991) Board of Education — Specific Powers.

COLO. REV. STAT. § 18-1-703 (1986) Use of Physical Force — Special Relationships.

COLO. REV. STAT. § 18-6-401 Child abuse (1991).

COLO. REV. STAT § 22-32-110- (2) (a) (III) (b).
People v. Jennings, 614 P.2d 276 (Colo. 1982).

CONNECTICUT

CONN. GEN. STAT. ANN. § 53a-18 (1990) Use of Reasonable Physical Force.

CONN. GEN. STAT. § 10-235 (a) Indemnification of teachers, board members and employees in damage suits; expenses of litigation.

Sansone v. Bechtel, 429 A.2d 820 (Conn. 1980).

Andreozzi v. Rubano, 41 A.2d 639 (Conn. 1958).

Swainbank v. Coombs, 115 A.2d 468 (Conn. Super. Ct. 1955).

Calway v. Williamson, 36 A.2d 377 (Conn. 1944).

O'Rourke v. Walker, 128 A. 25 (Conn. 1925).

Sheehan v. Sturgis, 2 A. 841 (Conn. 1855).

DELAWARE

DEL. CODE ANN. tit. 14 § 701 (1976) Authority of Teachers and Administrators to Administer Corporal Punishment.

DEL. CODE ANN. tit. 11 § 468 (1987) Use of Force by Persons with Special Responsibility for Care, Discipline or Safety of Others.

State v. Baccino, 282 A.2d 869 (Del. Super. Ct. 1971).

FLORIDA

FLA. STAT. ANN. § 230.23 (1990) Powers and duties of school board.

FLA. STAT. ANN. § 232.27 (West 1977 & Supp. 1987) Authority of Teacher.

FLA. STAT. ANN. § 228.041 Definitions.

FLA. STAT. ANN. § 231.085 Duties of Principal.

FLA. STAT. ANN. § 232.275 Liability of Teacher or Principal.

FLA. STAT. ANN. § 231.262 Complaints against Teachers and Administrators; Procedure.

Forehand v. School Bd. of Gulf County, 600 So. 2d (Fla. Dist. Ct. App. 1992).

B.R. v. Department of Health & Rehabilitative Serv., 558 So. 2d 1027 (Fla. Dist Ct. App. 1989).

W.M. v. Department of Health & Rehabilitative Serv., 553 So. 2d 274 (Fla. Dist. Ct. App. 1989).

B.L. v. Department of Health & Rehabilitative Serv., 545 So. 2d 289 (Fla. Dist. Ct. App. 1989), *Reh'g denied*, 553 So. 2d 1164 (1989).

B.B. v. Department of Health & Rehabilitative Serv., 542 So. 2d 1362 (Fla. Dist Ct. App. 1989).

M.J.B. v. Department of Health & Rehabilitative Serv., 543 So. 2d 352 (Fla. Dist. Ct. App. 1989).

Walker v. State, 501 So. 2d 156 (Fla. Dist. Ct. App. 1987).

Williams v. Cotton, 346 So. 2d 1039 (Fla. Dist. Ct. App. 1977).

GEORGIA

GA. CODE ANN. § 20-2-730 (1990) Policies and regulations on use of corporal punishment.

GA. CODE ANN. § 20-2-731 (1991) When and how corporal punishment may be administered.

GA. CODE ANN. § 20-2-732 (1991) When principal or teacher not liable for administering corporal punishment.

Crews v. McQueen, 385 S.E.2d 712 (Ga. Ct. App. 1989).

Mathis v. Berrien County Sch. Dist., 378 S.E.2d 505 (Ga. Ct. App. 1989), *cert. denied*, 190 Ga. Ct. App. 898 (1989).

Pennsylvania Millers Mut. Ins. Co. v. Crews, 361 S.E.2d 657 (Ga. Ct. App. 1987).

Maddox v. Boutwell, 336 S.E.2d 599 (Ga. Ct. App. 1985).

HAWAII

HAW. REV. STAT. § 298-16 (1988) Punishment of Pupils Limited.

HAW. REV. STAT. § 703-309 Use of Force by Persons with Special Responsibility for Care, Discipline or Safety of Others.

Shorba v. Board of Educ., 583 P.2d 313 (Haw. 1978).

Territory v. Cox, 24 Haw. 461 (1918).

Kahula v. Austin, 8 Haw. 54 (1890).

IDAHO

IDAHO CODE § 33-512 (Michie 1986) Government of Schools.

IDAHO CODE § 33-1224 (Mitchie 1991) Powers and duties of teachers.

Idaho State Bd. of Educ. IDAPA 08.02 Appx. I Statement by State Board of Education on Corporal Punishment (1978).

ILLINOIS

ILL. REV. STAT. ch. 122, para. 34-84a (Supp. 1987) Teachers shall Maintain Discipline.

ILL. REV. STAT. ch. 122, para. 24-24 (1989) Maintenance of Discipline.

23 ILL. ADM. CODE 1.280 (b) (1977) § 2-8.

Board of Educ. of Chicago v. Johnson, 570 N.E.2d 382 (Ill. App. Ct. 1991).

Roe v. Cradduck, 555 N.E.2d 1080 (Ill. App. Ct. 1990).

Illinois v. Wehmeyer, 509 N.E.2d 605 (Ill. App. Ct. 1987).

Swayne v. Board of Educ. of Rock Island Sch. Dist. No. 41, 494 N.E.2d 906 (Ill. App. Ct. 1986).

Board of Educ. of Sch. Dist. No. 131, Kane County v. State Bd. of Educ., 457 N.E.2d 435 (Ill. 1983).

Carter v. Board of Educ., 414 N.E.2d 153 (Ill. App. Ct. 1980) .

Eversole v. Wasson, 398 N.E.2d 1246 (Ill. App. Ct. 1980).

People v. Davis, 410 N.E.2d 673 (Ill. App. Ct. 1980).

Lowe v. Board of Educ. of City of Chicago, 395 N.E.2d 59 (Ill. App. Ct. 1979).

Baikie v. Luther High Sch. South, 366 N.E.2d 542 (Ill. App. Ct. 1977).

Gilliland v. Board of Educ. of Pleasant View, 365 N.E.2d 322 (Ill. 1977).

Welch v. Board of Educ., 358 N.E.2d 1364 (Ill. App. Ct. 1977).

Rolando v. School Directors, 358 N.E.2d 945 (Ill. App. Ct. 1976).

Kobylanski v. Chicago Bd. of Educ., 347 N.E.2d 705 (Ill. 1976).

Fender v. School Dist. No. 25, 347 N.E.2d 270 (Ill. App. Ct. 1976).

People v. Smith, 335 N.E.2d 125 (Ill. App. Ct. 1975).

Gordon v. Oak Park Sch. Dist. No. 97, 320 N.E.2d 389 (Ill. App. Ct. 1974).

INDIANA

IND. CODE ANN. § 20-8.1-5-2 (Burns 1985) Delegation of Authority.

IND. CODE ANN. § 35-41-3-1 Legal Authority.

Dayton v. State, 501 N.E.2d 482 (Ind. Ct. App. 1986).

Swingle v. State Employees' App. Comm'n, 452 N.E.2d 178 (Ind. Ct. App. 1983).

Indiana State Personnel Bd. v. Jackson, 192 N.E.2d 740 (Ind. 1963).

Vanvactor v. State, 15 N.E. 341 (Ind. 1888).

State v. Vanderbilt, 18 N.E. 266 (Ind. 1888).

Danenhoffer v. State, 69 Ind. 295 (1879).

Gardner v. State, 4 Ind. 632 (1853).

Cooper v. McJunkin, 4 Ind. 290 (1853).

Marlsbury v. State, 37 N.E. 558 (Ind. Ct. App. 1813).

IOWA

Iowa Code Ann. § 280.21 (1989) Corporal Punishment.

Iowa Code Ann. § 281-103.2-3 (1991) Ban on Corporal Punishment; Exclusions.

Iowa Code Ann. § 234.40 Child and Family Services: Corporal Punishment.

Northeast Community Educ. Ass'n v. Northeast Community Sch. Dist., 402 N.W.2d 765 (Iowa 1987).

Tinkham v. Kole, 110 N.W.2d 258 (Iowa 1961).

State v. Davis, 139 N.W. 1073 (Iowa 1913).

State v. Mizner, 50 Iowa. 145 (1878).

KANSAS

[No present law. During the 1991-92 legislative session, a bill limiting corporal punishment was passed in the House by a vote of 77-47 but failed in the State Senate on a vote of 20-20.]

KENTUCKY

Ky. Rev. Stat. Ann. § 161.180 (Baldwin 1987) Supervision of Pupils' Conduct.

Ky. Rev. Stat. Ann. 503.110 (Baldwin 1987) Use of force by person with responsibility for care, discipline or safety of others.

704 Ky. Admin. Regs. 7:056 (1992) Conditions for Administering Corporal Punishment.

Ky. Crime Comm. Commentary (1974).

Opp. Att'y. Gen. No. 78-704.

Opp. Att'y. Gen. No. 75-693.

Opp. Att'y. Gen. No. 69-534.

Opp. Att'y. Gen. No. 60-553.

Rone v. Daviess County Bd. of Educ., 655 S.W.2d 28 (Ky. Ct. App. 1983).

Owens v. Commonwealth, 473 S.W.2d 827 (Ky. 1971).

Carr v. Wright, 423 S.W.2d 521 (Ky. 1968).

LOUISIANA

LA. REV. STAT. ANN. tit. 17 § 223 (West 1982) Discipline of Pupils; Suspension from School, Corporal Punishment.

LA. REV. STAT. ANN. tit. 14 § 18 Justification; General Provisions.

LA. REV. STAT. ANN. tit. 17 § 81.6 Investigation of Employees.

LA. REV. STAT. ANN. tit. 17 § 416.1 Discipline of students; additional disciplinary authority.

Op. Att'y. Gen. No. 81-1355, (Jan. 8. 1982).

Haley v. McManus, 593 So. 2d 1339 (La. Ct. App. 1991).

Abraham v. Lafayette Parish Sch. Bd., 534 So. 2d 49 (La. Ct. App. 1988).

Harrell v. Daniels, 499 So. 2d 482 (La. Ct. App. 1986), *writ denied,* 501 So. 2d 214 (1986).

Gillory v. Ortego, 449 So. 2d 182 (La. Ct. App. 1984).

Geystand v. Louisiana Special Educ. Center, 415 So. 2d 409 (La. Ct. App. 1982).

Thomas v. Bedford, 389 So. 2d 405 (La. Ct. App. 1980).

McKenney v. Greene, 379 So. 2d 69 (La. Ct. App. 1980).

LeBlanc v. Tyler, 381 So. 2d 908 (La. Ct. App. 1980).

Thompson v. Iberville Parish Sch. Bd., 372 So. 2d 642 (La. Ct. App. 1979).

Allen v. LaSalle Parish Sch. Bd., 341 So. 2d 73 (La. Ct. App. 1977), *writ denied,* 343 So. 2d 203 (La. 1978).

Roy v. Continental Ins. Co., 313 So. 2d 349 (La. Ct. App. 1975), *writ denied,* 318 So. 2d 47 (1975).

Johnson v. Horace Mann Mutual Ins. Co., 241 So. 2d 588 (La. Ct. App. 1970).

Frank v. Orleans Parish Sch. Bd., 195 So. 2d 451 (La. Ct. App. 1967), *writ denied,* 197 So. 2d 653 (La. 1967).

Houeye v. St. Helena Parish Sch. Bd., 223 La. 966, 67 So. 2d 553 (La. 1953).

Watts v. Winn Parish Sch. Bd., 66 So. 2d 350 (La. Ct. App. 1953).

Burrage v. Gill, 130 So. 2d 857 (La. Ct. App. 1930).

MAINE

ME. REV. STAT. ANN. tit. 17A § 106 (1989) Physical Force by Persons with Special Responsibilities.

Comment to tit. 17A § 106 (1975).

ME. REV. STAT. ANN. tit. 20A § 4009 Civil Liability.

ME. REV. STAT. ANN. tit. 20A § 13020 (2)(A).

Winship v. Brewer Sch. Comm., 390 A.2d 1089 (Me. 1978).

McLaughlin v. Machias Sch. Comm., 385 A.2d 53 (Me. 1978).

Patterson v. Nutter, 7 A. 273 (Me. 1886).

MARYLAND

MD. EDUC. CODE ANN. § 7-305 (1988) Corporal Punishment; maintenance of order and discipline.

CODE OF MARYLAND REGULATIONS (1984 Supp.) tit. 13A § 08.01.06 Disciplinary Action.

[A new law forbidding corporal punishment is expected by June 1993.]

MASSACHUSETTS

MASS. ANN. LAWS ch. 71 § 37G (West 1977) Corporal Punishment Prohibited; Reasonable Force Allowed for Protection from Assault; Filing of Report.

School Comm. of Waltham v. Waltham Educ. Ass'n, 500 N.E.2d 1312 (Mass. 1986).

MICHIGAN

MICH. COMP. LAWS ANN. § 380.1312 (West Supp. 1988) "Corporal punishment" defined; infliction of corporal punishment by employee, volunteer, or contractor; exercise of necessary reasonable physical force; liability; violation; list of alternatives to use of corporal punishment; authority permitting corporal punishment void.

MICH. COMP. LAWS ANN. § 609.06 Authorized Use of Force.

Atkinson v. DeBraber, 446 N.W.2d 637 (Mich. Ct. App. 1989).

Tomszik v. State Tenure Comm'n, 438 N.W.2d 642 (Mich. Ct. App. 1989).

Willoughby v. Lehrbass, 388 N.W.2d 688 (Mich. 1986).

McIntosh v. Becker, 314 N.W.2d 728 (Mich. Ct. App. 1982).

MINNESOTA

MINN. STAT. ch. 127.45 (1990) Corporal Punishment.

MINN. STAT. ch. 609.379 Permitted actions.

Kruchten v. Reichert Bus Serv., Inc., 392 N.W.2d 50 (Minn. Ct. App. 1986).

Russell v. Special Sch. Dist., 366 N.W.2d 823 (Minn. Ct. App. 1985).

MISSISSIPPI

MISS. CODE ANN. § 37-11-53 (1991) Distribution of school district's discipline plan; content of plan; discipline conference; fines and penalties; recovery of damages.

MISS. CODE ANN. § 37-11-55 (1991) Code of student conduct.

MISS. CODE ANN. § 37-11-57 (1991) Immunity from liability for carrying out action in enforcing rules regarding control, discipline, suspension and expulsion of students.

MISS. CODE ANN. § 37-7-301 (g) School Board power to support Teachers and Principals for Discipline.

MISSOURI

MO. ANN. STAT. § 160.261 (Vernon Supp. 1988) Discipline, written policy established by local boards of education — contents — no civil liability for authorized personnel — spanking not child abuse, when — investigation procedure — officials falsifying reports, penalty.

MO. ANN. STAT. § 563.061 Use of Force by Persons with Responsibility for Care, Descipline or Safety of Others.

Opp. Att'y. Gen. No. 85 (Stevens 6-14-55).

Hudson v. Wellston Sch. Dist., 796 S.W.2d 31 (Mo. Ct. App. 1990).

Shepard v. South Harrison R-II Sch. Dist., 718 S.W.2d 195 (Mo. Ct. App. 1986).

Ortbals v. Special Sch. Dist. of St. Louis County, 762 S.W.2d 437 (Mo. Ct. App. 1983).

Streeter v. Hundley, 580 S.W.2d 283 (Mo. 1979).

Board of Educ. v. Shrank, 542 S.W.2d 779 (Mo. 1976).

Christman v. Hickman, 37 S.W.2d 672 (Mo. Ct. App. 1931).

Haycraft v. Griggsby, 88 Mo. App. 354 (1901).

State v. Boyer, 70 Mo. App. 156 (1897).

MONTANA

MONT. CODE ANN. § 20-4-302 (1991) Discipline and punishment of pupils — definition of corporal punishment — penalty — defense.

MONT. CODE ANN. § 20-5-201 (1987) Duties and sanctions.

MONT. CODE ANN. § 45-3-107 (1987). Use of force by parent, guardian, or teacher.

Donnes v. State ex rel. Superintendent of Pub. Instruction, 672 P.2d 617 (Mont. 1983).

State v. Straight, 347 P.2d 482 (Mont. 1959).

NEBRASKA

NEB. REV. STAT. § 79-4,140 (1988 Supp.) Corporal punishment; prohibited.

NEB. REV. STAT. § 28-1413.

NEB. REV. STAT. § 79-1234 Teacher's or administrator's certificate; revocation or suspension; grounds; notice and hearing; effect of failure to appear; order; reinstatement.

NEVADA

NEV. REV. STAT. ANN. § 392.465 (Michie Supp. 1987) Corporal punishment of pupils: Limitations; regulations; notice to parent or guardian.

NEW HAMPSHIRE

N.H. REV. STAT. ANN. § 627:6 (1986) Physical Force by Persons with Special Responsibilities.

N.H. State Bd. of Educ. Policy Statement No. 2865 (Oct. 27, 1975).

Kelley v. Johnson, C.A. No. 75-91, N.H. Dist. Ct., Feb. 12, 1976 (Clearinghouse No. 20,622).

Heritage v. Dodge, 9 A. 722 (N.H. 1886).

NEW JERSEY

N.J. STAT. ANN. § 18A:6-1 (West 1989) Corporal punishment of pupils.

Application of V.S., 609 A.2d 530 (N.J. Super. Ct. App. Div. 1992).

In re Cowan, 541 A.2d 298 (N.J. Super. Ct. App. Div. 1988).

Matter of Doyle, 493 A.2d 54 (N.J. Super. Ct. App. Div. 1985).

School Dist. of Borough of Red Bank v. Williams, 3 N.J. Admin. 237 (1981).

In re Tenure Hearing of Basil Fattell, 1977 N.J. Sch. L. Dec. 941 (N.J. Ed. Comm'r 1977).

In re Tenure Hearing of Samuel Ivens, 1977 N.J. Sch. L. Dec. 961 (N.J. Ed. Comm'r 1977).

NEW MEXICO

N.M. Stat. Ann. § 22-5-4.3 (1986) School discipline policies. S.B.E. Reg. No. 81-3 (1981)

Health Servs. Div. v. Temple Baptist Church, 814 P.2d 130 (N.M. Ct. App. 1991).

NEW YORK

N.Y. Penal Law § 35.10 (McKinney 1987) Justification; use of physical force generally.

8 N.Y.C.R.R. § 19.5 (1985) Prohibition of corporal punishment.

8 N.Y.C.R.R. § 100.2 General school requirements.

Cargill v. Sobel, 565 N.Y.S. 2d 902 (N.Y. App. Div. 1991).

Engel v. Sobel, 556 N.Y.S. 2d 179 (N.Y. App. Div. 1990).

Friedland v. Ambach, 522 N.Y.S.2d 696 (N.Y. App. Div. 1987).

Malte v. State, 510 N.Y.S.2d 353 (N.Y. App. Div. 1986), *appeal denied*, 507 N.E.2d 320 (N.Y. 1987).

Rodriguez v. Johnson, 504 N.Y.S.2d 379 (N.Y. Civ. Ct. 1986).

Pisculli v. Board of Educ., 492 N.Y.S.2d 807 (N.Y. App. Div. 1985).

In re Rodney C., 398 N.Y.S. 2d 511 (1977).

Bott v. Board of Educ., 360 N.E.2d 952 (N.Y. Fam. Ct. 1977).

Jerry v. Board of Educ., 376 N.Y.S.2d 737 (N.Y. App. Div. 1975) *appeal dismissed sua sponte*, 39 N.Y.2d 1057, 387 N.Y.S.2d 1034 (1976).

Hodgkins v. Board of Educ., 376 N.Y.S.2d 235 (N.Y. App. Div. 1975).

Clayton v. Board of Educ., 375 N.Y.S.2d 169 (N.Y. App. Div. 1975).

Hodgkins v. Central Sch. Dist. No. 1, 368 N.Y.S.2d 891 (N.Y. App. Div. 1975).

Op. Comm'r Educ. Dep't, 14 Educ. (1974).

Brown v. State 205 N.Y.S. 2d 73 (N.Y. Ct. Cl. 1960).

People *ex rel.* Ebert v. Baldini, 159 N.Y.S.2d 802 (White Plains City Ct. 1957).

In re Appeal of Louise Lehn, 72 St. Dep't (Educ.) 129 (1952).

People *ex rel.* Hogan v. Newton, 56 N.Y.S.2d 779 (City Ct. 1945).

People v. Mummert, 50 N.Y.S.2d 699 (Nassau County Ct. 1944).

Op. Educ. Dep't, 62 St. Dept. 172 (1940).

People v. Petrie, 198 N.Y.S. 81 (County Ct. 1923).

NORTH CAROLINA

N.C. GEN. STAT. § 115C-390 (1991) School personnel may use reasonable force.

N.C. GEN. STAT. § 115C-391 (1989) Corporal punishment, suspension, or expulsion of pupils.

N. C. GEN. STAT. § 115C-392 Appeal of disciplinary measures.

N. C. GEN. STAT. § 6-21.4 Allowance of counsel fees.

Gaspersohn v. Harnett County Bd. of Educ., 330 S.E.2d 489 (N.C. Ct. App. 1985), *rev. denied*, 335 S.E.2d 315 (1985).

State v. Pittard, 263 S.E.2d 809 (N.C. Ct. App. 1980), *rev. denied,* 267 S.E.2d 682 (N.C. 1980).

Kurtz v. Winston-Salem/Forsyth County Bd. of Educ., 250 S.E.2d 718 (N.C. Ct. App. 1979).

Thompson v. Wake County Bd. of Educ., 230 S.E.2d 164 (N.C. Ct. App. 1976), *rev'd on other grounds*, 233 S.E.2d 538 (N.C. 1977).

State v. Thornton, 48 S.E. 602 (N.C. 1904).

Drum v. Miller, 47 S.E. 421 (N.C. 1904).

State v. Long, 23 S.E. 431 (N.C. 1895).

State v. Pendergrass, 19 N.C. (2 Dev. & Bat.) 365 (1837).

NORTH DAKOTA

N.D. CENT. CODE § 15-47-47 (1989) Corporal Punishment — prohibited — guidelines.

N.D. CENT. CODE § 12.1-05-05 (1985) Use of force by persons with parental, custodial, or similar responsibilities.

Lithun v. Grand Forks Pub. Sch. Dist. No. 1, 307 N.W.2d 545 (N.D. 1981).

OHIO

OHIO REV. CODE ANN. § 3319.41 (Baldwin 1985) Use of force and infliction of corporal punishment on pupils.

OHIO REV. CODE ANN. § 3313.20 (Baldwin 1991) Rules and regulations; employee attendance at professional meetings, expenses.

OHIO REV. CODE ANN. § 2919.22 (Page Supp. 1988) Endangering children.

OHIO REV. CODE ANN. § 2901.01 (Page Supp. 1988) Definitions.

OHIO REV. CODE ANN. § 3301.0714 Education management system; annual report on each school district and each school building.

OHIO REV. CODE ANN. § 3319.088 Educational aides.

Op. Att'y Gen. No. 89-053 (1989).

Op. Att'y Gen. No. 73-129 (1973).

Op. Att'y Gen. No. 68-161 (1968).

State v. Cortner, 602 N.E.2d 779 (Ohio Ct. App. 1992).

Traub v. Wasem, # CA 16-85 (Ohio Ct. App. 1985).

State v. Albert, 456 N.E.2d 594 (Ohio County Ct. 1983).

State v. Hoover, 450 N.E.2d 710 (Ohio Ct. App. 1982).

Chrysinger v. Decatur, 445 N.E.2d 260 (Ohio Ct. App. 1982).

Dixon v. Youngstown City Board of Educ., C.A. No. C 73-1188 Y (N. Ohio Dist. Ct. July 23, 1975) (Clearinghouse Rev. No. 12,441).

Poole v. Young, A613952 (Cleveland Mun. Ct. 1962) (unreported).

State v. Lutz, 113 N.E.2d 757 (Ohio C.P. 1953).

Martin v. State, 21 Ohio Dec. 520 (Muskingum C.P. 1910), *affirmed mem.,* 102 N.E. 1132 (Ohio 1912).

Quinn v. Nolan, 4 Wkly. Law Bull. 81, 7 Ohio Dec. Reprint 585 (Ohio Super. Ct. 1879).

State v. Henderson, Ohio Dec. Misc. (Dayton) 353 (C.P. 1866).

OKLAHOMA

OKLA. STAT. ANN. tit. 70, § 6-114 (West 1989) Control and discipline of child.

OKLA. STAT. ANN. tit. 70 § 6-113.1 Materials on effective classroom discipline techniques to be furnished.

OKLA. STAT. ANN. tit. 21 § 643 (West 1983) Force against another not unlawful, when—Self-defense—Defense of property.

OKLA. STAT. ANN. tit. 21, § 843 (West 1983) Abuse of children— Penalty.

OKLA. STAT. ANN. tit. 21, § 844 (West 1983) Ordinary force as means of discipline not prohibited.

Holman v. Wheeler, 677 P.2d 645 (Okla. 1983).

Reirdon v. Wilburton Bd. of Educ., 611 P.2d 239 (Okla. 1980).

OREGON

OR. REV. STAT. ANN. § 339.250 (1987) Duty of pupil to comply with rules; discipline; written information on alternatative programs required.

OR. REV. STAT. ANN. § 161.205 (1985) When use of physical force is justifiable.

Thomas v. Cascade Union High Sch. Dist. No. 5, 724 P.2d 330 (Or. Ct. App. 1986).

Bethel Sch. Dist. No. 52, Lane County v. Skeen, 663 P.2d 781 (Or. Ct. App. 1983), *review denied* 670 P.2d 1033 (Or. 1983).

Lincoln County Sch. Dist. v. Mayer, 591 P.2d 755 (Or. Ct. App. 1979).

Barnes v. Fair Dismissal Appeals Bd., 548 P.2d 988 (Or. Ct. App. 1976).

Simms v. School Dist. No. 1, Multnomah County, 508 P.2d 236 (Or. Ct. App. 1973).

PENNSYLVANIA

24 PA. CONS. STAT. ANN. § 13-1317 (Purdon 1962 & Supp. 1989) Authority of teachers, vice principals and principals over pupils.

18 PA. CONS. STAT. ANN. § 509 (Purdon Supp. 1989) Use of force by persons with special responsibility for care, discipline or safety of others.

22 PA. CODE § 12.5 Corporal punishment.

Commonwealth v. Douglas, 588 A.2d 53 (Pa. Super. Ct. 1991).

Commonwealth v. Tullius, 582 A.2d 1 (Pa. Super. Ct. 1990).

Everett Area Sch. Dist. v. Ault, 548 A.2d 1341 (Pa. Commw. Ct. 1988).

Belasco v. Board of Pub. Educ., 510 A.2d 337 (Pa. 1986).

Blascovich v. Board of Sch. Directors, 410 A.2d 407 (Pa. Commw. Ct. 1980).

Board of Pub. Educ. v. Pyle, 390 A.2d 904 (Pa. Commw. Ct. 1978).

Penn-Delco Sch. Dist. v. Urso, 382 A.2d 162 (Pa. Commw. Ct. 1978).

Harris v. Commonwealth of Pa. Secretary of Educ., 372 A.2d 953 (Pa. Commw. Ct. 1977).

Landi v. West Chester Area Sch. Dist., 353 A.2d 895 (Pa. Commw. Ct. 1976).

Commonwealth v. Allen, 98 Dauph. 473 (Dauphin County C.P. 1976).

Commonwealth v. Sente, No. 40 (Clinton County C.P. Nov. 5, 1975).

Chodkowski v. Beck, 106 Pitts. L.J. 115 (1957).

Guerrieri v. Tyson, 24 A.2d 468 (Pa. Super. 1942).

Harris v. Galilley, 189 A. 779 (Pa. Super. 1937).

Rupp v. Zintner, 29 Pa. D. & C. 625 (Dist. Ct. 1937).

Commonwealth v. Yalk, 30 Luz. L. Reg. Rep. 173 (Luzerne County Ct. 1934).

Commonwealth v. Ebert, 11 Pa. D. 199, 3 Justice's L.R. 252 (Dist. Ct. 1901).

Commonwealth v. Seed, 5 Clark 78 (Pa. 1851).

Commonwealth v. Fell, 11 Haz. Pa. Reg. 179 (Pa. C.P. 1833).

RHODE ISLAND

R.I. GEN. LAWS § 40-11-2 (1990) Definitions.

R.I. GEN. LAWS § 9-1-31 (Michie Supp. 1988) Public school teachers, supervisors and administrators—Immunity from liability—Compensation for certain injuries—Duty upon school comittees and board of regents.

Barber v. Exeter-West Greenwich Sch. Comm., 418 A.2d 13 (R.I. 1980).

SOUTH CAROLINA

S.C. CONST. art. 1, § 15 Right of bail; excessive bail; cruel or unusual or corporal punishment; detention of witnesses.

S.C. CODE ANN. § 59-63-260 (Law. Co-op. 1977) Corporal Punishment.

Hendrickson v. Spartanburg County Sch. Dist., 413 S.E.2d 871 (S.C. Ct. App. 1992).

SOUTH DAKOTA

S.D. CODIFIED LAWS ANN. § 13-32-2 (1982) Physical punishment authorized when reasonable and necessary — Attendance at school functions away from premises — Authority of bus drivers.

S.D. CODIFIED LAWS ANN. § 22-18-5 (1990) Reasonable force used by parent, guardian, or teacher in correcting child.

S.D. CODIFIED LAWS ANN. § 26-10-1 Abuse of or cruelty to minors as felony.

TENNESSEE

TENN. CODE ANN. § 49-6-4103 (1983) Corporal punishment.

TENN. CODE ANN. § 49-6-4402 Corporal punishment.

TENN. CODE ANN. § 49-6-4203 Legislative intent.

TENN. CODE ANN. § 49-6-4104 (1979) Rules and regulations.

TENN. CODE ANN. § 49-6-4105 (Supp. 1988) Arrest and prosecution for injury to student.

TENN. CODE ANN § 49-6-4403 Penal and Reformatory Institutions - School Discipline rules and regulation.

TENN. CODE ANN. § 49-6-4404 (1980) Physical examination of student and student's remedies.

Hargrove v. York, ___ S.W.2d ___ (1993 TENN. APP. LEXIS 98).

Van Hooser v. Warren County Bd. of Educ., 807 S.W.2d 230 (Tenn. 1991).

Marlar v. Bill 78 S.W.2d 634 (Tenn. 1944).

State v. Von Stranz, 1 Tenn. Cas. (1 Shannon) 591, 3 Leg.Rep. 19 (Tenn. 1876).

Anderson v. State, 40 Tenn. (3 Head) 455 (Tenn. 1859).

TEXAS

TEX. EDUC. CODE ANN. § 21.912 (Vernon 1987) Duties of Professional Employees; Liability.

TEX. EDUC. CODE ANN. § 13.906 (Vernon) Student Teachers.

TEX. PENAL CODE ANN. § 9.62 (Vernon 1974) Educator—Student.

Commentary to Tex. Penal Code Ann. § 9.62.

Burton v. Kirby, 775 S.W.2d 834 (Tex. Ct. App. 1989).

Mathis v. Angleton Indep. Sch. Dist., TEA Docket No. 146[2]-RI-780 (Tex. Comm'r. Educ. 1982).

O'Haver v. Blair, 619 S.W.2d 467 (Tex. Ct. App. 1981).

Hogenson v. Williams, 542 S.W.2d 456 (Tex. Civ. App. 1976).

Harwell v. State, 258 S.W. 814 (Tex. Crim. App. 1924).

Dill v. State, 87 Tex. Crim. 49 (Tex. Crim. App. 1920).

Harris v. State, 203 S.W. 1089 (Tex. Crim. App. 1918).

Gibson v. State, 203 S.W. 1091 (Tex. Crim. App. 1918).

Prendergast v. Masterson, 196 S.W. 246 (Tex. Civ. App. 1917).

Wilson v. State, 190 S.W. 155 (Tex. Crim. App. 1916).

Ely v. State, 68 Tex. Crim. 562 (Tex. Crim. App. 1912).

Greer v. State, 106 S.W. 359 (Tex. Crim. App. 1907).

Stephens v. State, 68 S.W. 281 (Tex. Crim. App. 1902).

Howerton v. State, 43 S.W. 1018 (Tex. Crim. App. 1898).

Thomason v. State, 43 S.W. 1013 (Tex. Crim. App. 1898).

Kinnard v. State, 33 S.W. 234 (Tex. Crim. 1895).

Whitley v. State, 25 S.W. 1072 (Tex. Crim. App. 1894).

Spear v. State, 25 S.W. 125 (Tex. Crim. App. 1894).

Smith v. State, 20 S.W. 360 (Tex. Crim. App. 1892).

Hutton v. State, 5 S.W. 122 (Tex. Ct. App. 1887).

Bolding v. State, 4 S.W. 579 (Tex. Ct. App. 1887).

Metcalf v. State, 17 S.W. 142 (Tex. App. 1886).

Bell v. State, 51 Am. Rep. 293 (Tex.App. 1885).

Dowlen v. State, 14 Tex. App. 61 (1883).

Stanfield v. State, 43 T. 167 (1875).

UTAH

UTAH CODE ANN. § 76-2-401 (1978) Justification as defense—When allowed.—Conduct which is justified is a defense to prosecution for any offense based on the conduct.

UTAH CODE ANN. § 53A-11-801 Physical Restraint Guidelines: Definitions.

UTAH CODE ANN. § 53A-11-802 Prohibition of corporal punishment-Use of reasonable and necessary physical restraint or force.

UTAH CODE ANN. § 53A-11-803 Investigation of complaint - Confidentiality - Immunity.

UTAH CODE ANN. § 53A-11-804 Liability.

Rowley v. Board of Educ. of Duchesne County Sch. Dist., 576 P.2d 865 (Utah 1978).

VERMONT

VT. STAT. ANN. tit. 16, § 1161a (Supp. 1988) Discipline.

VT. STAT. ANN. tit. 33, § 3503 Child Care Facilities: Corporal punishment prohibited.

Shields v. Gerhart, 582 A.2d 153 (Vt. 1990).

Melen v. McLaughlin, 176 A. 297 (Vt. 1934).

Lander v. Seaver, 32 Vt. 114 (1859).

State v. Williams, 27 Vt. 755 (1855).

VIRGINIA

VA. CODE ANN. § 22.1-279.1 (Supp. 1989) Corporal punishment prohibited.

WASHINGTON

WASH. REV. CODE ANN. § 28A.87.230 (Supp. 1989) Interfering by force or violence with any administrator, teacher, classified employee, or student unlawful.

WASH. REV. CODE ANN. § 28A.87.231 (Supp. 1989) Intimidating any administrator, teacher, classified employee, or student by threat of force or violence unlawful.

WASH. REV. CODE ANN. § 28A.87.232 (Supp. 1989) Violations under RCW 28A.87.230 and 28A.87.231—Disciplinary authority exception.

WASH. REV. CODE ANN. § 9A.16.100 (West 1988) Use of force on children—Policy—Actions presumed unreasonable.

WASH. ADMIN. CODE § 180-40-235 (1987-88) Discipline—Conditions and limitations.

Commentary to § 180-40-235.

WASH. ADMIN. CODE § 180-40-240 (1986) Discipline—Grievance procedure.

Mott v. Endicott School Dist. No. 308, 713 P.2d 98 (Wash. 1986).

Simmons v. Vancouver School Dist. No. 37, 704 P.2d 648 (Wash. Ct. App. 1985).

Sargent v. Selah School Dist. No. 119, 599 P.2d 25 (Wash. Ct. App. 1979).

WEST VIRGINIA

W. VA. CODE § 18A-5-1 (1988) Authority of teachers and other school personnel; exclusion of pupils having infectious diseases; suspension or expulsion of disorderly pupils; authority of principals to administer corporal punishment.

W. VA. CODE § 18A-5-8 Authority of certain aides to excerise control over pupils.

W. VA. CODE § 29-12-5a Liability insurance.

Mingo County Equal Opportunity Council v. State Human Rights Comm'n., 376 S.E.2d 134 (W. Va. 1988).

West Virginia Dep't of Human Resources v. Boley, 358 S.E.2d 438 (W. Va. 1987).

Mullins v. Kiser, 331 S.E.2d 494 (W. Va. 1985).

Smith v. West Virginia State Bd. of Educ., 295 S.E.2d 680 (W. Va. 1982).

WISCONSIN

WIS. STAT. ANN. § 118.31 (West Supp. 1988) Corporal Punishment.
Satutory Note to § 118.31.
WIS. STAT. ANN. § 939.45. Privilege.
Steber v. Norris, 206 N.W. 173 (Wis. 1925).

WYOMING

WYO. STAT. § 21-4-308 (1986) Punishment and disciplinary measures; denial of diploma or credit.
WYO. STAT. § 6-2-503 (1988) Child abuse; penalty.
WYO. STAT. § 14-3-202 (1986) Definitions.
State v. Spiegel, 270 P. 1064 (Wyo. 1928).